Coordinated Activity Programs for the Aged

A How-To-Do-It Manual

Albert G. Incani
Barry L. Seward
Jack E. Sigler

AHA ®

American Hospital Publishing, Inc.,
a wholly owned subsidiary
of the American Hospital Association

Library of Congress Cataloging in Publication Data

Incani, Albert G.,   1910-
    Coordinated activity programs for the aged.
    Reprint. Originally published: Chicago: American
Hospital Association, 1975.
    Includes bibliographies.
    "Catalog no. 175124"—T.p. verso.
    1. Nursing homes—Recreational activities.   2. Aged—
Recreation.   3. Occupational therapy.   4. Volunteer
workers in long-term care facilities.   I. Seward,
Barry L., 1941-   . II. Sigler, Jack E.   III. Title.
[DNLM: 1. Aged.   2. Recreation. WT 30 I36c]
RA999.R42I53 1985   362.1'6   85-1276
ISBN 0-939450-60-7

Catalog no. 175124
© 1975 by
American Hospital Publishing, Inc.,
a wholly owned subsidiary
of the American Hospital Association

AHA is a service mark of American Hospital Association
used under license by American Hospital Publishing, Inc.

Printed in the U.S.A.
M94-6M-6/75-4334
1M-1/85-0076
1M-11/86-0167

Contents

List of Figures

Preface

This book is a how-to-do-it manual. Like most manuals, it is designed for application in as nearly an ideal setting as possible. However, the manual is just as effective and the steps described just as important in a difficult setting as they are in the ideal. You will, of course, have to adapt the recommendations to fit your setting—BUT PLEASE DO NOT SKIP ANY OF THE STEPS.

The activity program upon which the manual is based was developed at Swope Ridge Health Care Center, which was designated by the U.S. Department of Health, Education, and Welfare as a Region VII Long-Term Care Training Center. The program was tested at several other nursing homes in the Kansas City area. To a considerable extent, the program described is a product of the particular environment in which it was developed. Therefore, an understanding of the basic philosophy of Swope Ridge would be helpful in understanding the particular goals of the program.

Because there are many differences between the acutely ill patient and the chronically ill patient, caring for the latter requires a totally different approach—and the adoption of a special philosophy.

The acute patient is often in danger of losing his life. He knows he must give up his independence— rely on others—to get well. So he is submissive and regards his doctor and nurse as all-knowing and all-powerful.

The chronically ill patient, on the other hand, is seldom in immediate danger of losing his life, nor is he totally incapacitated, but his length of stay is long. Because he knows the doctor and the nurse cannot perform miracles for him, he is unlikely to obey instructions without question. He needs considerable social and emotional support—and so do the members of his family, who often feel both guilty and concerned that he is institutionalized.

Personnel must, therefore, deal with psychological as well as physical needs, and be concerned with each patient's interests and activities as well as his care. Close patient-staff relationships become unavoidable; in fact, they are desirable. And because the resident is not confined to bed—nor even to his room—he is encouraged to regard it only as a place to sleep and to strive for maximum independence.

In short, a nursing home should be a real home —providing residents with life's normal satisfactions. At Swope Ridge we try to make group living like family life. There is respect for individual preferences as well as consideration for others. There is warmth, understanding, and concern for the morale and welfare of each person. All of us, working together, try to convey this to residents and their relatives.

We recognize that to make life worth living takes more than a beautiful building, or the best service and care, or a good recreation program. We believe residents need a feeling of belonging and purposeful activity if there is to be any happiness in their lives. So each resident is given a voice in the home's affairs and is encouraged to voluntarily perform some function useful to others.

A residents' council, consisting of a chairman, a secretary, and the heads of seven committees, meets regularly with the administrator. Their responsibilities range from suggesting menus and welcoming visitors to planning weekly religious services and stimulating participation in various activities.

No resident is permitted to regard himself as a terminal patient. Instead, he is encouraged to develop an optimistic outlook—to feel that he has come to Swope Ridge to live, not to die.

Physical therapy has been an integral part of Swope Ridge's program of total care for many years—and with dramatic results. Because nothing is so discouraging to a person as the loss of the skills he once had, efforts to rehabilitate physical and mental abilities or to slow their degeneration help to develop the positive point of view.

The activity department plays a key role, coordinating and integrating within the pattern of care such activities as occupational therapy, educational courses, and religious and recreational events. With the help of a federal grant, we have documented the best ways of doing this in the hope that these techniques and training programs will be beneficial to you and to elderly persons everywhere.

Our basic purpose—in this as in everything we do at Swope Ridge—is to remotivate our residents toward purposeful living. We teach them to accept their chronic disabilities and show them how they can continue their pursuit of lifelong interests. We adapt activities to capabilities—always focusing on rehabilitation, *not* vegetation.

One of the keys to the successful development of this program has been the team of consultants, who effectively shared ideas with each other as well as with Barry Seward, administrator, Swope Ridge Health Care Center, and project director, and with Jack Sigler, director, Program on Aging, Institute for Community Studies, Kansas City, MO. The result has been the growth of a program that is truly a blend of the ideas, purposes, and techniques of the various disciplines involved. The contributions of the following consultants are gratefully acknowledged:

Chaplaincy services: Warren Dentler, United Ministries Chaplain, University of Missouri at Kansas City

Occupational therapy: Julie Eagle, OTR, occupational therapist, Swope Ridge Health Care Center, Kansas City, MO

Educational services: Bill Jessee, Ed.D., associate professor, Counselor Education, University of Missouri at Kansas City

Volunteer services: Marie Santee, director of voluntary services, Veterans Administration Hospital, Kansas City, MO

Recreational therapy: Richard Stracke, chief, Recreation Therapy, Veterans Administration Hospital, Kansas City, MO

Gratitude is also expressed to the staff of Swope Ridge, the many community volunteers who contributed much to make this a successful program, and Earl Welty and his staff at the Office of Aging, Department of Community Affairs, State of Missouri, who made this project possible through Grant Number 1009-67-A, under the Title 3 program of the Older Americans Act.

Albert G. Incani
Executive Director
Swope Ridge Health Care Center

chapter *1*
The Case for Coordinated Activities

It is well known that activity programs are used as constructive outlets for the energies of youth throughout the country. Schools have long included them in their curriculums and are increasingly supporting these programs, even in the summer months, when school traditionally is not in session. Workers in inner-city areas have also turned to activity programs as one way to provide for the development of constructive expression. Activity programs are evidenced in other forms also. Retirement communities, hotels, and vacation resorts offer activity programs as inducements to prospective clients. Churches too include activities in their programs.

In the chapters that follow, you will read about an activity program that has been specifically planned, developed, and tested for use in institutions that serve the aged and the chronically ill— service to whom is both challenging and rewarding.

Aging as a Point of Focus

Even a cursory review of current literature discloses society's increased awareness of that segment of the population usually referred to as the aged. This increased awareness of and interest in the problems of the aged are based upon a number of trends.

One such trend is the obvious increase in the total number of persons of all ages. The accelerating rate of population growth means that there are more older people now and, perhaps more important, that even more people are approaching advanced age. The significance of these increased numbers is considerably enhanced by another characteristic of society—the lengthening life expectancy. In 1850 the average length of life in the United States was a little over 38 years; by 1956

*Starbeams, *Kansas City Star*, Aug. 6, 1970, with permission.

figure 1
percent of population
with chronic conditions,
by selected age groups

	Selected Age Groups		
	45-64	65-74	75+
Percent with one or more chronic conditions	65.8	80.4	87.4
Percent with chronic conditions that limit activity	19.8	42.6	60.5

Reprinted from *Economics of Aging: Toward a Full Share in Abundance*, Part I, Survey Hearing. Hearing before the Special Committee on Aging, U.S. Senate, Washington, DC, Apr. 29-30, 1969, p. 204.

the average had increased to 69.7 years;[1] and by 1968 to 70.2 years.[2] Thus, far greater proportions of the expanding population are living to reach advanced age.

Modern medical and dietary technology makes it possible to avoid many of the ills that in the past have prevented people from attaining their allotted life span. Current and future efforts to overcome heart disease, cancer, and stroke promise to add even more years to life expectancy. Although medicine is helping people to "not die sooner," other scientific efforts are under way that have the potential of lengthening the life span. The net result is, and for many years will continue to be, that more and more people will reach that advanced stage in life now called old age.

Considering the present state of knowledge, the ability to live longer is not necessarily a blessing. Although it is true that modern medicine has been able to give the prospect of longer life, the health system has not as yet been able to make much progress toward prevention or alleviation of accumulated chronic conditions that are the consequence of prior illness and living conditions. The longer one lives, the greater the opportunity for some chronic illness or disability to develop. Among older people today, chronic conditions are quite prevalent, especially those chronic conditions that limit activity (figure 1, above). Unless some new preventive techniques are developed, the chances are that the proportion of older people with chronic conditions will increase.

Another trend that is cause for increased concern with the aged involves retirement. In 1900 only about one-fourth of those over 65 were retired.

Today, the situation is quite different: 80 percent of the people in this age bracket are retired,[3] and 87 percent receive Social Security payments.[4] What is more, there is a growing trend toward "early" retirement, that is, retirement prior to age 65.

Retirement, whether early or late, creates for many a dual loss. The more obvious is the usual immediate decrease in income. It is common for this loss of income to create the necessity for decreased activity. Decreased activity, under certain circumstances, can lead to isolation, loneliness, and deteriorating physical powers. Completing the vicious cycle, unless intervention occurs these conditions often necessitate increased medical expenditures, and so even less money is available for other activities.

Another loss that accompanies retirement is less obvious but often more upsetting than the loss of income: the loss of work roles and child-rearing roles. Retirement is a period characterized by severe adjustments in the worker's identity. Reports of feelings of uselessness, lack of purpose, and "just being in the way" are not uncommon. Loss of sleep and other physical and psychological reactions may occur.[5] When coupled with the problems associated with living on a fixed income during times of inflation, retirement poses a considerable threat to the older worker unless he has been planning for it.

Neither loneliness nor isolation is confined to the older person, but the likelihood of occurrence is greater for him. Poorer physical condition, decreased income, loss of family and friends through

[1]Coe, R. M., and Wesson, A. F. *Sociology of Medicine*. New York City: McGraw-Hill, 1970.
[2]U.S. National Center for Health Statistics. Life Tables. In: *Vital Statistics of the United States, 1968* (Vol. II. Mortality, Part A, Sec. 5). Washington, DC: U.S. Government Printing Office, 1968, pp. 1-8.

[3]U.S. Congress. Senate. Special Committee on Aging. *Employment Aspects: Hearing before the Special Committee on Aging (Economics of Aging, Part 9)*. Washington, DC: U.S. Government Printing Office, Dec. 18-19, 1969, p. 1310.
[4]U.S. Department of Health, Education, and Welfare. *Facts on Aging* (AOA Pub. No. 146). Washington, DC: U.S. Government Printing Office, May 1970, p. 9.
[5]Price, D. My year alone. *Modern Maturity*. 13:9, June-July 1970.

migration or death, and alienation from many of today's concerns all contribute to the older person's physical and social isolation.[6]

As you have been reading this, you may have been saying, "It doesn't have to be like this." It doesn't! And it shouldn't be! It is obvious that not all older people fit into such a black, problematic picture. Why? How are they different? What has been done to prevent such "normal" developments as decreased physical and mental health, increased loneliness, and loss of purpose? Finding answers to these and other questions, and the development of programs and techniques of intervention, is the job of each of us. We must ask ourselves, "What do I have to offer aging and aged persons?"

Nursing Homes as a Point of Focus

Since people in nursing homes are, by definition, ill and/or chronically disabled, why should so much attention be given to an activity program for them? The answer to this question lies at the heart of the philosophy upon which the program described in this book is based.

A fundamental precept of this program is that "man" is a total blending of the various aspects of life: physical, psychological, and social. The use of "nursing home" as a label for institutions that care for the chronically ill and elderly focuses the attention of both providers and receivers of services upon the *physical* aspects of care. As a consequence, the *psychological* and *social* aspects of programming, if offered at all, are usually considered as extra services rather than the vital remaining pieces of the total therapeutic milieu. However, effective care cannot be obtained unless all three aspects of life are a part of the total care package.

By the time a person enters a nursing home, the social and psychological aspects of his life have undergone as much change as his physical condition. From the standpoint of respect, leadership, and decision making (in his own family at least), the nursing home resident now finds himself in a position in which he no longer controls the family money, his opinion is no longer sought, he has probably lost his spouse, his children are away from home and are living independent lives, and he is physically powerless and almost completely dependent upon the nursing home staff. Feelings of

rejection and uselessness are common, and "everyone" tells him to relax, rest, and let someone else do it.

Resting, relaxing, and acting lazy serve a useful purpose for the working, active person. For the elderly retired person, and especially the nursing home resident, the same resting behavior more often than not creates more harm than good. As one elderly resident once said, "Rest? Rest from what? I'm not tired. I haven't done a damn thing for months!" In order that rest might regain some of its physical, psychological, and social value, the nursing home resident must reengage in some form of activity related to the "normal" needs and processes of living.

In other words, the nursing home resident is faced with a variety of role changes and conflicts. The resident may well remember past physical prowess and social status, but declining health and the bewildering social changes and loss of status that accompany retirement reflect to a great extent the effects of advancing age in our society. The resident may well have to accept physical and social loss, but frequently he does not recognize or show the effects of age in his ability to think, carry on conversations, and perform other mental functions.

The activity theory of aging postulates a close positive relationship between level of activity and degree of life satisfaction.[7] A complete nursing home care program should include attempts to rehabilitate and to make use of skills in all three aspects of its residents' lives: physical, psychological, and social. To do this, the nursing home must recognize that it has the responsibility of serving the totality of a person's needs. Recognizing all aspects of the individual is another way of saying that the administrators and staff must keep in mind the humanity of the resident. It must also be recognized that the home has the responsibility of serving a resident's "needs," which may be different from "wants." A patient may not want to become involved with living—indeed, he may actually want to die. A total program accepts the challenge of remotivation of the desire to live.

It is obvious that to accomplish this admittedly difficult task the personnel of all departments within the nursing home must share the same ulti-

[6]White House Conference on Aging. *Retirement Roles and Activities: Background and Issues*, by G. F. Strieb. Washington, DC: U.S. Government Printing Office, Feb. 1971.

[7]Lemon, B. W., and others. An exploration of activity theory of aging: Activity types and life satisfaction among in-movers to a retirement community. *Journal of Gerontology.* 27:511, Oct. 1972.

mate goals. This includes mutual respect for other personnel and recognition of the problems of others who are primarily serving different aspects of the resident's needs. All personnel in the home must work together on a *coordinated* basis if they are to create an integrated therapeutic environment.

Activity Programs: Application and Value in Nursing Homes

Until recent years, society accepted the conditions of old age and chronic illness as the time at which one stops participating in most activities. Society in general had not yet become cognizant of the fact that although the physical body may deteriorate because of time and/or chronic illness, the need for normal life activities continues.

Yet all human beings—young or old, sick or well, living independently or in a nursing home—have the same *basic* needs. Although the needs may vary in intensity and form, surely the nursing home resident does not want—and should not be allowed —to sit and vegetate until he dies. The resident must be encouraged to learn to live with his age and physical condition and to continue to take part in purposeful activities. If a nursing home is truly a place to live, it must offer opportunities for resident participation in the "normal activities of life." This means that the home is responsible for providing warm interpersonal relationships; meaningful activities; opportunities for cultural, social, and spiritual satisfaction; and a sense of responsibility and participation.

The belief that residents of nursing homes need more than medical and nursing care is becoming more widespread among leading doctors and administrators. According to Dukelow, "An underlying necessity which surpasses all others, and without which everything becomes as dust and ashes in the mouths of our elder citizens, is the need for happiness and recognition. Without this, food, shelter, clothing, medical and dental care, essential as these are, are not enough. The emotional needs of the elderly are exactly the same as those felt by every human being at every age. They may be intensified in the later years, but they are basically the same. They are but two—to be loved and to be needed."[8]

Modern administrators realize that in addition to good medical and nursing care they must provide a wide range of activities to meet the psychological needs of each person in order to provide a total care program. Miller states that "the administration of a progressive nursing home is committed to the encouragement and development of the imaginative recreation service."[9]

The psychological needs of residents can be fulfilled in full or in part through resident involvement in such "life activity" programs as work, recreation, education, religion, self-maintenance, and social interpersonal relationships. The following list of interrelated general objectives was developed in cooperation with consultants specializing in the sociology of aging, occupational therapy, therapeutic recreation, education, chaplaincy, and volunteer services:

- Develop self-confidence and wholesome life attitudes
- Stimulate and encourage social interaction
- Encourage self-motivation
- Enable the resident to be useful, serving, and loving
- Afford health maintenance and rehabilitation
- Develop interests and skills
- Provide for spiritual satisfaction
- Provide intellectual stimulation
- Stimulate creativity and expression
- Develop substitutes or outlets for continuation of occupational or vocational abilities

Everyone should come to recognize and understand both the intrinsic and extrinsic values that can be derived from participation in meaningful activities that enable each resident to live as fully and independently as his desires and capabilities allow. In "The Triumph of Aging," Byrnes pointed out that Benjamin Franklin wrote his autobiography when over 80, Stradivarius was still making his violins up to the age of 93, Grandma Moses began painting at 79, and Michelangelo completed his paintings on the ceiling of the Sistine Chapel when he was over 80.[10] Such genius may not be found among the residents in your nursing home, but many residents may have talents and abilities that they no longer are given the opportunity to use. They also may not be given the opportunity to

[8]Dukelow, D. A. Changing attitudes toward the elderly. *More Life for Your Years: A Fact Sheet for Older Persons from the American Medical Association.* 8:2, Oct. 1969.

[9]Miller, D. Nursing home setting. How the administrator relates to the recreation program. *Parks and Recreation.* 11:38, Jan. 1967.
[10]Byrnes, H. W. The triumph of aging. *Adult Leadership.* 17:388, Mar. 1969.

learn new skills. When this occurs, one aspect of living—the possibility of continued growth and achievement—has been suppressed.

The primary purpose of an activity program is to pull residents out of withdrawal or seclusion and to remotivate them to function in the normal routines of living. The activity director must be flexible and open to the contributions of various specialties, such as recreational therapy, occupational therapy, education, institutional chaplaincy, and volunteer services. He should not have an allegiance to only one field of specialization but should strive for what is best for each situation.

Many specific programs encompass several interrelated aspects of the six life activity areas: work, recreation, education, religion, self-maintenance, and social interpersonal relationships. In addition, information and knowledge that have been gained from various professional fields can be used to more effectively meet the needs of the resident. A basic concept of total care is recognition that a person must be considered as an integrated whole rather than a compartmentalized entity divided along departmental or disciplinary lines.

Because activities are now included as an integral part of total care programs, they are being used as one criterion for recognizing high-quality care. Until recently, patient activities were never considered an important adjunct to active *treatment* programs that encourage restoration to self-care; hence they were almost nonexistent in institutions. At last there is a trend that ascribes positive values to this field, just as they are ascribed to nursing, dietary, physical therapy, and other services.

It has been amply demonstrated that the presence of an activity program in an institution favorably influences the party responsible for the resident. Admitting a relative into a nursing home is a major decision in the lives of most adult children.

It is natural for the adult children to discuss this event with friends and to give them the reasons for making the decision they did—in order to gain reassurance that they have done the right thing. They want—even need—to feel that their decision was based upon the fact that their loved one is now receiving a type of care that they would be unable to offer at home. In addition to good health care, clean rooms, and good meals, high on the list of "talking points" are the potential activities available that provide pleasure, happiness, and companionship. In the process of seeking reassurance from others, the responsible party is trying hard to sell the nursing home of his choice to others in the hope that they will agree that he made the correct decision. The net result, of course, is word-of-mouth advertising, long accepted as being the most effective and acceptable form of public relations for nursing homes.

The remaining chapters are based upon the assumption that you already know what an activity program is and that you are interested in how to establish such a program. Consequently, these chapters are organized in a step-by-step manner and are to be considered as a guide to organizing and operating such a program. A further assumption is that you are considering the establishment of a full-scale coordinated activity program. It is possible, of course, that you are not in a position to make such a full commitment to the program at this time. Some adaptation will therefore be necessary in order to maximize the benefit from the program suggested here. Most important, however, *the concepts and principles described here remain the same whether or not a full-scale program is to be established.* Any deviation should be in the degree of formality only and not in the principles involved.

chapter 2
Organizational Considerations

To attain the various objectives set forth in chapter 1, it is important that a sound preliminary organization be established. In this chapter several organizational components and considerations are discussed. Also included are examples of workable forms and outlines that are helpful in establishing the proper organization. The first section focuses on the physical facilities needed to house the program. This is followed by a discussion of budgeting, staffing, training, policies and procedures, and records and reports.

Physical Facilities

An activity program requires space to operate. The lack of any obviously available space has, unfortunately, kept many nursing home administrators from seriously considering the establishment of an activity program. But this need not be the case, because *some* space can be found. Various types of potential space can be adapted for activities. Each administrator must survey the institution to determine availability of space and its current use.

Some nursing homes are fortunate enough to have built into their physical plant specific types of activity areas such as an auditorium, chapel, craft room, game room, library, kitchen, classrooms, and lounges. Others have constructed multipurpose areas in order to achieve maximum utilization of space. Institutions not having such elaborate areas can consider using lounges, waiting rooms, dining rooms, television rooms, enclosed porches, wards, lobbies, kitchens, foyers, garages, and other areas. A program can generally be developed within an existing institution if other departments or services cooperate in making space available when it is not otherwise in use.

Contrary to usual thinking, activities need not be held indoors. Often, under a desirable climate, outdoor areas can be put to good use. Lawns, porches, and patios are the most frequently used. Picnic areas, sports and games areas, and gardens are among other outdoor areas sometimes developed.

Other required aspects of physical facilities include a good communications system, proper lighting, and good ventilation. Although storage space for equipment is often a problem, it is imperative that storage space of some type be available.

Last but not least, the activity director himself should have an office that provides an atmosphere conducive to planning and coordination.

Budgeting

A definitive departmental budget must be developed. There is the obvious need to determine the amount of money that can be expended for the activity program. Furthermore, other benefits are also derived from the budgeting process. For instance, developing a justification for the budget provides one of the first occasions for detailed organizing and planning—you must have some idea of what you want to do before you can develop a meaningful budget. Presenting the justified budget to the administration provides an opportunity not only to establish monetary limits but also to develop a real sense of commitment to the project on the part of the administrator.

The budget should include such basic considerations as the cost of salaries (including fringe benefits and payroll taxes), supplies (including equipment and consumable supplies), and staff development.

Staffing

Staffing, as the term is used here, involves the total process of selecting and training personnel. The capabilities of the personnel selected determine how successfully a program accomplishes its objectives and how broadly conceived these objectives are.

The actual staffing pattern employed depends upon the particular circumstances of the institution. Many nursing homes employ only one full-time person. Others have several employees on the activity staff. In some cases, a part-time person may be the only economically feasible alternative; for example, two or more institutions may hire one individual to share time between them. There is a growing trend for administrators to seek the services of a professional consultant when a nonprofessional is charged with directing an activity program.

So many factors must be considered that it is wise for the administrator to determine which staffing alternatives best fit the needs of the institution. For illustrative purposes, the procedures used for the selection and training of a full-time professional activity director are described. With slight variations, the same procedures can be followed for other staff positions.

There are five steps in the staff selection process: (1) developing a job description, (2) developing job requirements, (3) recruiting applicants, (4) interviewing applicants, and (5) making the selection.

Job Description

A job description (figure 2, page 12) is prepared for the purpose of describing the responsibilities of a particular position. Writing out the description clarifies the responsibilities for both the employer and the employee. It also serves as an aid in recruiting and interviewing. Information should include the name and address of the organization, name of the department, job title, name of the immediate supervisor, duties, education and experience requirements, skills, aptitudes, abilities, salary range, fringe benefits, and other information and comments deemed desirable.

Job Requirements

The job requirements statement is used as an aid during interviews. It describes the desirable characteristics of the person who is to carry out the duties referred to in the job description. The job requirements should be stated in terms of what the applicant *can* do (figure 3, page 14) and in terms of what he *will* do (figure 4, page 15). "Can do" characteristics relate to health and physical status, ability, knowledge, and special requirements. "Will do" characteristics concern interests, motivation, personal adjustment, and attitude.

Recruiting and Interviewing

The recruitment process should be started *only* after the job description and job requirements have been established. Whether or not there are eligible candidates within the organization, it is desirable to look to external sources also.

Newspaper advertising can be considered for professional and nonprofessional positions. Weekend papers generally produce better results than daily editions.

Such ads (figure 5, page 16) are more effective if they are highlighted by noting something unique or challenging about the organization and/or the department, such as "Build your own program" or "Can you interest the elderly?" If a professional person is desired, ads can be placed with professional journals and universities that have recreational or occupational therapy curriculums. Professionals in the vicinity should be made aware of the position available, for they can refer candidates (both professional and nonprofessional) to your organization.

The nursing home administration likely has set up methods for learning about the training, experience, background, intelligence, physical condition, aptitudes, skills, and moral and emotional character of applicants. If not, the following tools are means of gaining this information:

- Application blank
- Interview, aided by completed job requirements statements
- References from previous employers, schools attended, credit sources, and police department
- Physical examination

Selection and Training

After the information listed above has been gained and the findings thoroughly considered, the selection of the desired applicant can be made with greater assurance. Following selection, the employee should receive a thorough orientation. The orientation should include information about the history, philosophy, and policies of the organization; a tour of the facility; and introduction to any staff and volunteers who may already be associated with the department, other department heads, staff, and residents. In addition to the initial tour, sufficient time should be arranged for a thorough familiarization with all other services offered by the institution and for becoming acquainted with the residents.

An activity director should be capable of providing in-service classes for staff, but he, too, must have opportunities for continued growth. Attending outside classes in related subject areas is helpful not only to the individual but also to the organization. Workshops, institutes, seminars, field trips, and conferences provide further opportunities for growth and development. Adequate books, journals, and references as well as periodic contact with professional consultants are beneficial.

These costs are investments that pay dividends immediately as well as in the future.

Policies and Procedures

Many employees, both administrators and staff, frequently enter into a working relationship with only vague and little understood ideas about how things are to be done. Establishing policies and procedures goes a long way toward eliminating the confusion of ad hoc decision making and the uncertainty and inefficiency that accompany this type of decision making. Written policies and procedures also provide a sense of continuity; add simplicity in the long run; and increase staff understanding while reducing potential conflict.

Policies

Policies are general statements that guide the thinking of personnel. Before an activity program is begun, policies should be established in line with the objectives; policies can be changed and added as the need arises. A review of policies at least annually is desirable.

Every institution has its own policies, *whether they are written or not.* Having policies in writing provides greater assurance that all personnel will understand them and will carry out their responsibilities within these boundaries. Such policy statements have further advantages, because they enable an administrator to delegate responsibility more confidently.

Certain policies will vary in different institutions, but there is a need for common policies on certain subjects (figures 6 through 8, pages 16 through 20). Since every institution operates differently, examples of policies should not necessarily be copied verbatim. Those shown here are offered primarily as guides.

Procedures

By spelling out specific plans for achieving objectives, procedures ensure that responsibilities will be carried out in a uniform manner. As methods are improved, procedures can be revised and updated. Like policies, the procedures followed in each institution differ according to need.

Records and Reports

Among the least understood and most often resisted aspects of operating a good activity program are the need for and use of proper record keeping.

As will be seen by the many types of records discussed in the following sections, there are several purposes for these records. Some of the records are needed to legally protect all concerned. Others are useful in evaluating the success of a given program or activity to determine whether it should be repeated. Still others are used to better meet the needs of residents or to justify requests for budget modifications or renewal. The forms discussed below are included to acquaint the reader with this particular part of the job responsibility. The discussion includes an explanation of who might complete the form, what is to be recorded, and when and where the information is to be recorded.

Social History

At the time of admission the admitting officer should question the family, or other responsible person or persons, regarding the past social history (figure 9, page 20) of the new resident. This information can be used to better plan for meeting the needs and interests of the resident. Certain information gained from the social history must, of course, remain confidential.

Initial Evaluation

A staff member should go to the room of each new resident as soon after his admission as possible, to welcome him and inform him of the activity program and other services. This will enable the staff to draw some conclusions about the resident's capabilities and interests (figure 10, page 21), in order to get him involved in the nursing home immediately. Both the early meeting and the early involvement are intended to assist the resident to adjust to the new surroundings as rapidly as possible.

Interest Questionnaire

Another interest finder is the interest questionnaire (figure 11, page 22). The resident should be visited by a volunteer or other person, who gathers information on the likes and dislikes of the resident. The questionnaire helps the staff know the resident better and assists in planning for him.

Tally Sheet for Interest Questionnaire

The tally sheet (figure 12, page 24) can be kept up to date by volunteers after they visit residents for the purpose of completing the interest questionnaire. It is a valuable instrument in determining some of the general interests of the total resident population. It also provides an accessible file of information on individuals interested in particular activities. Through its use, residents can be notified of particular activities in which they had indicated interest, they can be approached if they have offered assistance, and their suggestions can be evaluated.

Progress Notes

Progress notes (figure 13, page 27) can be maintained on all residents or only on residents receiving therapy or other special services. These confidential reports are prepared in private by a staff member working with, or assigned to observe, the resident. The notes provide information for the medical staff, other professional services, or another facility if the resident is transferred. Certain information can be shared with the family.

Activity Report

The activity report (figure 14, page 28) is a tool for evaluating activities and the reactions of residents to these activities in order to improve the quality of programming. Staff members or volunteers who conducted the program can record general information and attendance; report their program ratings and reactions; and offer any comments, suggestions, or criticisms. Filing these reports with the description of the program is helpful in improving the activity if it is conducted again.

Daily Attendance Record

Attendance should be recorded (figure 15, page 29) during each activity. Residents' names are written in the left column at the time of their first visit, and the activity checked. Any other activities attended during the day can then be indicated by placing checks in the appropriate box. By adding the columns, a total daily attendance can be recorded. Adding the names produces the total number of different persons, called "initial visits" or "unduplicated count," seen during the day.

Monthly Attendance Record

At the end of each day, or preferably following each activity, a staff member can add daily attendance to the monthly attendance record (figure 16, page 30). The initial visits (as referred to in the daily attendance record) should be recorded and circled above the total attendance figure in each appropriate box. This provides a quick reference as well as necessary information for reports.

Out-Trip Approval Form

The out-trip approval form (figure 17, page 31) is first utilized by staff members to list the names of residents who are interested in attending a particular outing. A copy is given to the nursing director so that she can request permission from each resident's physician. At that time, the physician or nurse can also indicate precautions required for those approved to go.

A final list is prepared for the nursing staff members so that they can make preparations prior to the trip. It also informs them of which residents in their area will be gone. This list not only is informative to nursing but also provides protection for the activity staff against taking residents outside the facility without authorization.

Photo Releases

The resident photo release (figure 18, page 32) indicates that permission is given by the resident to include him in photographs illustrating activities at the facility. The authorized photo release (figure 19, page 32) is used when a resident is not capable of giving this permission by himself; the family or assigned responsible person may grant this authority. In order to protect the resident, the personnel, and the organization, a release must be signed before any picture is taken.

Residents' Charges

An itemized list of charges (figure 20, page 32) to be added to residents' accounts should be prepared monthly by the assigned staff member. Charges can be noted at the time of a service or a purchase. Charges for craft supplies can be added at the end of the month by taking the information from the form used to record costs at the time materials are purchased. All residents' charges should then be forwarded to the accounting department.

Debit Slip

The debit slip (figure 21, page 33) is used to record small amounts of income. To maintain good bookkeeping records and to avoid confusion in petty cash records, a completed debit slip accompanied by the monies should be transferred to accounting and credited to the department.

Credit Slip

The credit slip (figure 22, page 33) is used to record expenditures taken from petty cash. When petty cash is nearly depleted, the credit slips can be exchanged for the amount of expenditures. This will bring the total petty cash fund back to its original amount.

Sign-out Sheet

The sign-out sheet (figure 23, page 33) is used to record items that are loaned out. The information requested on the form is completed at the time an item is borrowed. In this way, a record of the location of an item is maintained.

Inventory—Supplies and Equipment

A physical inventory of supplies and equipment should be recorded on the appropriate forms (figures 24 and 25, page 34) at regular intervals. These provide control and aid in determining needs.

Donations

When a donation of cash, supplies, or equipment is received, a receipt (figure 26, page 35) should be given to the donor. If possible, the dollar value of the donation should be shown. A copy should be kept by the department to provide a record of cash or items received.

Charges for Craft Supplies

The staff member who starts a resident on a new project should complete the information requested on the appropriate form (figure 27, page 35). This keeps other staff and volunteers informed and can be used to complete residents' charges at the end of the month.

Work Schedule

The director schedules the days and hours he or she and other staff members will be working. A schedule (figure 28, page 35) should then be posted for easy access.

Party Form

Staff members should use a form (figure 29, page 36) in preparation for parties. It is a helpful device for making sure nothing is overlooked. Assignments can be listed, so that each person will know the function he is to perform.

Purchases

A purchase requisition (figure 30, page 37) is used to request supplies from various departments or from commercial sources in advance of the date wanted. Examples are food items and housekeeping supplies.

**figure 2
example of
job description**

NAME AND ADDRESS OF ORGANIZATION

Department: Activities Department

Job Title: Activity Director

Responsible to: Administration

Duties:
Plans, organizes, and directs an activity program for residents.
Develops activities in accordance with residents' needs, interests, and
capacity to participate.
Provides opportunities for recreation, work, education, religion,
self-maintenance, and social and interpersonal relationships.
Selects and supervises all personnel within the department.
Develops and maintains a good relationship with contacts within the
community.
Is responsible for the preparation of departmental records and reports.
Develops effective communication with other department heads.
Coordinates the program with other nursing home services.
Contributes to the educational program of the facility by providing orientation
classes related to the area of diversional activities.
Is responsible for training assistants and volunteers in methods of remotivating
residents to participate in normal daily living activities.
Plans, organizes, and directs a volunteer services program designed to improve
the total care of the residents.
Is responsible for the recruitment, screening, orientation, placement, and
recognition of the volunteers.
Maintains reports and records in relation to the volunteer program.
Performs related duties as required.

Education: Bachelor's degree from an accredited college or university with a
major in recreational therapy, occupational therapy, or a field of study
appropriate to a specialized activity function within the program or, for
those employed full-time in the profession, a total of seven years of
academic training and full-time experience in related work.

Experience: Minimum of one year successful full-time paid experience in a
related setting.

Skills, Aptitudes, and Abilities:
Must have activity skills in several recreational areas and working knowledge
of such activities as arts and crafts, domestic activities, dance, dramatics,
games, gardening, music, sports, and other hobbies and special interest
areas.
Must be familiar with methods and principles of leadership.
Must have some understanding of the mechanical functioning of the body in
order to prevent aggravation of residents' physical condition.
Must be familiar with basic medical terminology.
Must have understanding of human motivation and behavior.
Must be physically capable of participating in and conducting semiactive
programs.

**figure 2
(cont.)**

Must be capable of moving relatively light equipment in preparation for a variety of activities.

Must be willing to work with the aged and chronically ill.

Must have tactful, pleasant, and friendly approach in dealing with residents, staff, guests, and individuals within the community.

Must be alert for signs of unfavorable symptoms, such as fatigue and irritability.

Must use sound judgment and considerable initiative in adapting to given situations.

Hours: Personal schedule must conform to needs of the job. Hours may be from 9 to 5 or 12:30 to 8:30, depending upon the schedule of resident activities. Occasional weekends and holidays.

Salary Range: (as determined)

Fringe Benefits: (as determined)

figure 3
example of
list of job
requirements: can do

INTERVIEWING AID: CAN DO CHARACTERISTICS
DIVERSIONAL ACTIVITY DIRECTOR

NAME_____   DATE_____

Job Requirements	Available Information	Needed Information	Summary of Significant Information
Health and Physical Status Age: 25 to 50 (preferred range) Sex: Male or female Height and weight: In proportion Attractive appearance, well groomed Stamina to withstand long hours and emotional tension Pleasant speaking voice Good health (no chronic illness)			
Ability and Knowledge Activity skills Leadership skills and ability Familiarity with basic medical terminology Understanding of human motivation Ability to plan and direct activities Ability to select and train employees Ability to speak before groups Ability to prepare business letters Supervisory abilities Ability to maintain proper records and reports College degree in related field (or combination of five years of experience and education)			
Special Influencing Conditions Must be able to maintain regular schedule Must be able to work irregular hours occasionally Must be free from family interference Must have transportation available at all times			

**figure 4
example of
list of job
requirements: will do**

INTERVIEWING AID: WILL DO CHARACTERISTICS
DIVERSIONAL ACTIVITY DIRECTOR

NAME _____ DATE _____

Job Requirements	Available Information	Needed Information	Summary of Significant Information
Interests and Motivation Interest in nursing home atmosphere Interest in older and chronically ill persons Interest in working with people Interest in recreation, education, and other life activities Motivation to accept leadership responsibility High degree of initiative **Personal Adjustment** Requires flexibility regarding ability to work both alone and as part of a group Requires high degree of emotional and physical stability Requires high degree of responsibility, including keeping confidences Requires ability to accept authority and exercise it judicially **Attitude** Friendly, understanding attitude toward others Ability to maintain objective viewpoint Lack of bias toward persons of other race, creed, and so forth Favorable attitude toward new ideas Enthusiastic approach to life			

**figure 5
example of
recruitment
advertisement**

ACTIVITY DIRECTOR
with
imagination,
patience, and
resourcefulness.
To head
comprehensive program
for senior citizens.

Opportunity to develop
recreational,
educational, and
religious activities
as a part of a dynamic
total care program.

(Name of organization)
(Address of organization)
(Telephone number)

**figure 6
example of
personnel policies**

PERSONNEL POLICIES

Beginning Work

The first three months of employment are a probationary period. For various reasons, the probationary period may be extended.

Orientation

All new employees will receive an orientation to the department and a tour of the primary areas within the facility. All employees will also receive a copy of the general personnel policies and will be expected to read and remember these policies.

Work Schedule

Personnel will be assigned on a 5-day, 7½-hour schedule, with the exception of weekends. The shifts are 8:30 to 4:30 and 12:30 to 8:30 weekdays, 8:30 to 4:30 Saturday, and 9:30 to 4:30 Sunday.

Dress and Appearance

Uniforms are not required. Employees are therefore requested to wear appropriate dress. Absolute personal cleanliness is a must. Employees should be well groomed and should not wear too much makeup or jewelry. Name tags must be worn.

Attendance

Employees should be prepared for work on time and should avoid unnecessary absence. Good attendance is required for pay raises and promotions.

Personal Property

The safekeeping of personal property is the owner's responsibility. Money or valuables should be carried or locked in a safe place.

**figure 6
(cont.)**

Phone Calls and Mail
Phones should not be used for personal calls, and personal mail should not be received at this address.

Resignation
Two weeks' notice is expected in order to find a qualified replacement.

Discharge
Immediate discharge without notice may result from behavior that may offend or injure others.

Time Cards
An employee's paycheck depends on how many hours his time card shows he worked. It's up to every employee to keep his card accurate.

**figure 7
example of
department policies**

DEPARTMENT POLICIES

Program Development
Initiating, coordinating, and developing the activities are the responsibility of the activity director or his/her designee.

No payments are made to entertainers, speakers, or others who perform services for residents. These occasional volunteers must be recruited on a nonremunerated basis.

Posters or flyers announcing the highlights of the day's activities are posted on the central bulletin board. Announcements are made over the public address system at intervals of one-half hour before, one-quarter hour before, and at the time the program is scheduled to begin.

Activities must be supervised. At least one staff member or volunteer must remain in the activity area during a program.

Attendance
Residents capable of attending activities should be invited. Positive encouragement and motivation are frequently necessary.

Preferably, nursing staff members should assist residents to the activity area. If their cooperation is not received, activity staff members and/or volunteers should do so.

A program at bedside is encouraged for residents who cannot or will not attend other activities. Staff or volunteers should visit the rooms regularly to provide opportunities at the mental and physical level of the resident.

Attendance is recorded during each activity on the daily attendance record and the total figure indicated on the program report and monthly report.

Program Records and Reports
Daily activities are evaluated on the first day of each month. Occasional activities are critiqued immediately after the activity.

Appearance of Area
Staff members are responsible for the appearance of activity areas. They must keep office, storage, and other areas in order, including equipment, supplies, desks, and file cabinets.

Everything belonging to the department is assigned to a particular area. Everything must be returned to its assigned location, unless prior approval to do otherwise has been received.

**figure 7
(cont.)**

Sale of Products

Residents are permitted to sell products they have made. They may do this individually or request that the department display them in a sale case. All profits are awarded to the resident.

Staff Meetings

There is a weekly department meeting. Anyone not present is expected to review the minutes of the meeting and complete any given assignments.

Professional staff meetings are held weekly between the directors of nursing, physical therapy, social service, and activities, to discuss goals, progress, and methods of better serving each resident.

Resident Evaluation and Progress

Newly admitted residents will receive a visit from the activity director, staff member, or volunteer. This contact is for the purpose of welcoming the resident and gaining pertinent information to assist in evaluating his/her main interests and capabilities in order to plan involvement as quickly as possible.

Doctors requesting specific therapy for a resident will be asked to complete a prescription. This program will be under the supervision of a registered therapist. At other times, the activity director will attempt to involve residents in activities that meet their needs and interests. The activity director may consult with the nursing director and/or directors of other services.

Progress notes are not prepared on all residents. Written reports of resident progress in therapeutic activities are made, and bedside involvement is frequently registered. Notes requested by administrators or doctors will be maintained.

**figure 8
example of
administrative
policies**

ADMINISTRATIVE POLICIES

Purchasing

All purchases must be approved by the administration except when specified types of purchase authority are designated to another individual.

Inventory Control

Inventory of all supplies and equipment is checked and recorded quarterly.

Public Relations

All materials for publication, including articles and photographs, must be approved by the administrator.

Photographs taken of residents, whether for publication or not, must be approved in writing by the resident or, if the resident is not capable of making mature judgment, by his family. This procedure is not necessary if pictures are taken on a Polaroid® camera (and thus there are no negatives) and the photo is given to the resident.

Key Control

Only authorized persons receive keys, or access to keys, to designated areas. No one should have personal keys made without authorization.

Forms Control

All forms must be approved by the administration before being duplicated. A number will be assigned to each form.

**figure 8
(cont.)**

Donations

Useful donations are accepted and solicited for use in the nursing home. Cash donations are accepted only by the administration, and a receipt is given immediately to the individual or group. Thank you notes are sent to individuals, groups, or organizations making donations.

Safety

Unsafe conditions should be reported immediately. Sound judgment should be used so as not to endanger residents. All accidents, no matter how small, should be reported. In case of fire, the procedures outlined in the fire emergency plan should be followed.

Maintenance and Housekeeping

All maintenance and housekeeping requests are to be in writing on the prescribed "Work Order Request" form. In the event of an emergency requiring immediate attention, (name) or (name) should be contacted.

Reports

From time to time reports are requested from all departments. Department heads are charged with the responsibility of seeing that the reports are completed and returned at the proper time.

Time Cards and Time Sheets

Department heads prepare new time cards for their department on or before the last day of the pay period. Time sheets are to be submitted to the business office on the last day of each pay period.

Transportation

Resident outings receive priority for use of the organization vehicle. At other times its use may include pickups and deliveries. Approval for other uses must be granted by the administrative staff.

Personnel asked by the activity director to use their own cars for business will receive reimbursement. All use of personnel vehicles must be authorized. If residents are being transported, liability insurance is automatically transferred to the automobile. To receive the reimbursement, it is necessary for the employee to indicate the mileage and to include his signature on the form provided.

Charges to Residents

Residents are charged for supplies purchased by the department. Donated supplies are given to residents without charge. Methods of payment are included in the procedures.

Correspondence

Letters confirming program arrangements made by telephone, in person, or by earlier written correspondence should be mailed to guests at least one week in advance. Thank you letters or notes should be sent to individuals or groups not more than two weeks from the time of the activity.

Use of Area and Property

The activity area and property are for primary use of the residents. Reservations for use of the activity area are made to the activity director. Equipment may be borrowed at the discretion of the activity director if it is not needed for resident use at that time.

**figure 8
(cont.)**

If personnel wish to take books or other materials home, permission of the activity director must be obtained. A posted sign-out sheet indicating the name of the borrower, the time borrowed, date taken, and date returned is to be completed.

Petty Cash

A petty cash fund of $25 is established for easing the "red tape" of small purchases. A credit slip must be completed for all disbursements. The amount recorded on credit slips, plus the amount of cash, must always equal $25.

**figure 9
example of
social history**

SOCIAL HISTORY

Name——————————————— Date admitted——————

Address——————————— City——————— State————

Previous address (that is, other states)——————————————

Date of birth——————— Place of birth——————— Sex————

Medical

Name of physician——————— Office address————— Phone————

Background leading to admission in re social or home care problems

————————————————————————————————

Physical handicaps————————————————————————

Emotional stability———————————————————————

Past psychological treatment, Length of——————————————

Injuries and medical record—————————————————————

Has patient ever received physical therapy, occupational therapy, or speech therapy?——————— If so, where and when?———————————

Has patient ever been seen by a social worker?——————— If so, where and when?————————————————————————————

Under what circumstances could patient go home?————————

————————————————————————————————

Expected length of stay—————————————————————

Financial

Is patient on Medicare?——————— Other medical plan?——————

Does patient have personal income?——————— Social Security?————

Pension?——————— Insurance?———————

Does patient, family, or trust handle finances?——————————

Who is directly financially responsible for patient?————————

What effect does the above have on patient going home?——————

Family

Is spouse living?——————— If living, give wedding anniversary.————

Spouse's name——————————— Occupation————————

Was patient visited regularly during other hospital stays?—————

Will patient be visited regularly here?———————————————

Is patient able to talk on the telephone?——————————————

Does patient like to write?——————— Receive mail?———————

**figure 9
(cont.)**

Religion
Is patient a member of a church or a temple?_____ If yes, give name
and address. _____
Give name of priest, minister, or rabbi. _____
Has patient been active (present and past) in any church related activities?
_____ If yes, give details. _____

Recreation
Cultural interests (literature, music, theater, art)?_____
If yes, be specific. _____
Hobbies (crafts, gardening, collecting things, reading)?_____
If yes, be specific. _____
Sports (spectator or participant)?_____ If yes, be specific._____
_____
Games (any kind)?_____ If yes, be specific. _____
Club/fraternal memberships?_____ If yes, be specific. _____
Travel?_____ If yes, be specific. _____

Education
Elementary school_____ High school_____ College_____
Give name of last school. _____
Graduate degrees?_____ Technical training?_____

Occupation
Previous occupations _____

Habits
Does patient customarily take afternoon naps?_____
Customary bedtime hours_____ Is patient restless at night?_____
Does patient have any food preferences?_____
Usual mealtime hours_____
List any other habits you feel are important. _____

**figure 10
example of
initial evaluation**

INITIAL EVALUATION

Name of resident_____ Contacted by_____
Date_____ Religion_____

Medical diagnosis/pertinent information:

Family and background information:

Former occupations, hobbies, interests, skills:

Observations on resident's condition (physical condition, mental attitude, mood):

Other pertinent information:

Thoughts on follow-up contacts. How can diversional activities serve resident's needs and desires?

figure 11
example of
interest questionnaire

INTEREST QUESTIONNAIRE

Name—————————————————— Room——————————

Arts and Crafts
Do you enjoy working in arts and crafts?————— List kinds (painting, sewing, and so on). ———————————————

Audiovisual Activities
Do you enjoy watching movies?————— Slides?————— On what subjects?

Do you have slides that you would show here?————— If yes, on what subjects? ———————————————

Continuing Education
Would you enjoy lectures or demonstrations presented on various interesting subjects?————— What topics would be of interest to you?—————

Would you take part in discussion groups?—————
Would you enjoy taking part in classes (government, music appreciation, travel, and so on)?————— List subjects. —————

Would you enjoy exhibits (art, antiques, and so on)?—————
Do you have anything you would like to exhibit?—————
Give details. —————

Dance
Do you like watching others dance?—————
Have you ever danced?————— Ballroom————— Square—————

Domestic Activities
Do you like doing domestic work?————— Cleaning————— Sewing—————
Cooking————— Ironing————— Washing dishes————— Other (list).

Dramatics
Do you enjoy plays and skits?————— Would you take part in a play group?—————

Entertainment
Do you enjoy quiz programs similar to those seen on TV ("What's My Line?," "Two for the Money," "Password," and so on)?—————
Would you participate on a panel for one of these programs?—————
Do you enjoy watching variety entertainment?—————
What type do you most enjoy?—————

Games
Do you like playing table games?————— List kinds (cards or dice, parlor games, and so on). —————

figure 11 (cont.)

Literature
Do you enjoy reading?_____ Fiction_____ Nonfiction_____
Prose_____ Verse_____
Have you ever written prose?_____ Verse?_____ If yes, explain.

_____

Nature Activities
Do you have an interest in nature?_____ List kinds of interest (gardening, weather forecasting, lapidary work, and so on). _____

Do you have any plants in your room?_____ If no, would you like any? _____ Anything specific?_____

Music
Do you like music?_____ List kinds (popular, classical, gospel, and so on). _____

Do you like to sing?_____ Community singing_____ Chorus_____
Solo_____
Do you play a musical instrument?_____ If so, what?_____

Occupation
What kind of work did you do?_____
Would you be interested in carrying on your skills?_____ Would you like to participate in a program in which you could make money?_____

Parties and Celebrations
Do you enjoy parties?_____ Would you enjoy participating on a party committee to plan games?_____ Entertainment?_____
Decorations?_____ Refreshments?_____

Religion
Would you like to attend church services?_____
Catholic_____ Protestant_____ Jewish_____
Would you like to take part in a Bible study group?_____

Residents' Council
Would you like to help make our nursing home a better place by taking an active part in deciding its present and future?_____ Would you partici-pate on one or more of the following committees? Recreation/Hobbies_____
Religion_____ Education_____ Welcoming_____ Food_____
Building/Grounds_____

Service Projects
Would you like to do meaningful things for others?_____ If yes, would you volunteer to make things for others?_____ Sew cancer dressings?_____
Provide telephone reassurance for the homebound?_____ Teach young people or adults in basic education areas?_____ Contribute to charity fund drives?_____ Other? Be specific. _____

figure 11 (cont.)

Trips

If you could, would you like to participate in outings to various places of interest, including churches, museums, concerts, nightclubs, theaters, sporting events?_____ What places would you most enjoy visiting? Be specific.

_____

Other Activities

Do you like to write letters?_____ If so, do you need assistance?_____

Do you like to read newspapers and magazines?_____ If so, do you need assistance?_____ Would large-print reading material be helpful?_____

Do you like to talk on the telephone?_____ Do you frequently receive calls?_____

Are you registered to vote?_____ If so, where?_____

If not, would you like to be?_____

Do you plan to invite friends or relatives to visit with you?_____

Attend meals?_____ Attend activities?_____

Do you have any food or drink preferences?_____ Specify._____

Do you have friends or relatives who entertain?_____

Show home slides?_____ Collect things?_____ Other?_____

Have we missed anything?

We would like this completed questionnaire to summarize your interests. If you think the story is incomplete, please add your comments here.

figure 12 example of tally sheet for interest questionnaire

TALLY SHEET FOR INTEREST QUESTIONNAIRE
Month————————————Year————

Arts and Crafts (List kinds suggested and indicate number of times.)

_____ _____ _____
_____ _____ _____
_____ _____ _____

Audiovisual Activities (List subjects suggested and indicate number of times.)

_____ _____ _____
_____ _____ _____
_____ _____ _____

Continuing Education (Use checks in boxes and indicate topics underneath.)

Lectures/Demonstrations	Discussion Groups	Classes	Exhibits

**figure 12
(cont.)**

Dance (Use checks.)

Ballroom (Social)	Square	Folk	Other (Name)

Domestic Activities (Use checks.)

Cleaning	Sewing	Cooking	Ironing	Washing Dishes	Other (Name)

Dramatics (List persons interested.)

Reading	Acting	Direction/Production

Entertainment (List persons offering to participate on quiz panels.)

_____ _____ _____

_____ _____ _____

_____ _____ _____

(List types of variety entertainment suggested and indicate number of times.)

_____ _____ _____

_____ _____ _____

_____ _____ _____

Games (List kinds suggested and indicate number of times.)

_____ _____ _____

_____ _____ _____

_____ _____ _____

Literature (List names.)

Reading

Fiction	Nonfiction	Prose	Verse

Writing

Prose	Verse

Nature Activities (List kinds of interest suggested and check number of times.)

_____ _____ _____

_____ _____ _____

_____ _____ _____

**figure 12
(cont.)**

Music (List names.)

Solo	Chorus	Chorus	Chorus

Name and Instrument	Name and Instrument

Occupation (List names and type of work done.)

_____ _____ _____
_____ _____ _____
_____ _____ _____

Parties and Celebrations (List names.)

Games	Entertainment	Decorations	Refreshments

Religion (Use checks to indicate number of each.)

Catholic	Protestant	Jewish

Residents' Council (List names.)

Recreation/Hobbies	Religion	Education	Welcoming	Food	Building/Grounds

Service Projects (List names and projects.)

_____ _____ _____
_____ _____ _____
_____ _____ _____

Trips-Outings (List trips and number of times suggested.)

_____ _____ _____
_____ _____ _____
_____ _____ _____

**figure 13
example of
progress notes**

PROGRESS NOTES

Name_____ Room No._____

Medical Diagnosis/Information_____

_____

Date	Remarks

**figure 14
example of
activity report**

ACTIVITY REPORT

Activity

Date_____ Time_____ Place_____

Leadership

Resident Attendance_____ Total Attendance_____ Initial Visits_____

Program Rating:	**Excellent ← 5**	**4**	**3**	**2**	**1 → Poor**
Appropriateness	—	—	—	—	—
Preliminary Planning	—	—	—	—	—
Atmosphere	—	—	—	—	—
Presentation and Communication	—	—	—	—	
Variety and Balance	—	—	—	—	—
Continuity	—	—	—	—	
Flexibility	—	—	—	—	—
Interesting and/or Challenging	—	—	—	—	—
Use of Equipment Time and Leadership	—	—	—	—	
Caliber and Attitude of Program Guests	—	—	—	—	—
Resident Reaction	—	—	—	—	—
Extent of Participation (not only physical)	—	—	—	—	—
Tenor of Group	—	—	—	—	—
Enthusiasm	—	—	—	—	—

Comments

Suggestions

figure 15
example of
daily
attendance record

DAILY ATTENDANCE RECORD

Date _____ Name	Arts and crafts, a.m.	Committee meetings	Education classes	Book reading	Room visits and craft cart	Arts and crafts, p.m.	Jewish services	Protestant services	Catholic services	Communions	Therapeutic activities	Other (morning)	Other (afternoon)	Other (evening)
Total														

**figure 16
example of
monthly
attendance
record**

MONTHLY ATTENDANCE RECORD

Month_____Year_____

Activity	1	2	3	4	5	6	7	8	9	10	11	12	13	14	15	16	17	18	19	20	21	22	23	24	25	26	27	28	29	30
Arts and crafts, a.m.																														
Committee meetings																														
Education classes																														
Book reading																														
Room visits and craft cart																														
Arts and crafts, p.m.																														
Jewish services																														
Protestant services																														
Catholic services																														
Communions																														
Therapeutic activities																														
Other, morning																														
Other, afternoon																														
Other, evening																														
Initial attendance																														
Total attendance																														

**figure 17
example of
out-trip approval form**

OUT-TRIP APPROVAL FORM

The following persons wish to attend an outing to

_____,

which will be held on_____, _____.

The group will leave the premises at ____:____, and will return at about

____:____. All persons listed below must be approved for outings by the

attending physicians. Please note any precautions.

	Name	Approved	Precautions
1.			
2.			
3.			
4.			
5.			
6.			
7.			
8.			
9.			
10.			
11.			
12.			

**figure 18
example of
resident photo release**

PHOTO RELEASE

I am willing to be included in photos illustrating activities at _____

_____

Signed_____

Date_____

**figure 19
example of
authorized
photo release**

PHOTO RELEASE

I give permission for _____ to be

included in photos illustrating activities at _____

_____

Signed_____

Relationship to resident_____

Date_____

**figure 20
example of
residents'
charges form**

CHARGES

Date	Resident	Room	Description	Amount
1.				
2.				
3.				
4.				
5.				
6.				
7.				
8.				

(Name and address of organization)

_____

Approved by

**figure 21
example of debit slip**

————————— 19——

Debit _____

Item_____ Amount_____

Department (or account number)_____

Person receiving money_____

Signature_____

**figure 22
example of credit slip**

————————— 19——

Credit _____

Item_____ Amount_____

Name_____

Department_____

**figure 23
example of
sign-out sheet**

SIGN-OUT SHEET

Date	Name	Item	Approved by	Date returned

figure 24
example of
supply inventory

SUPPLY INVENTORY

Date_____

Standard supply	Quantity on hand	Description of item	Location of item	Reorder

figure 25
example of
equipment inventory

EQUIPMENT INVENTORY

No. _____

Quantity	Description/ ID no. of item	Date acquired	Purchased or donated	Depreciation schedule	Location of item	Date of last inventory

**figure 26
example of
receipt for donation**

RECEIPT FOR DONATION

No._____   Date_____

Received of_____

_____ Dollars
                                          (or)

_____

By_____

**figure 27
example of
charges form
for craft supplies**

CHARGES FOR CRAFT SUPPLIES

Date	Name	Description (item, color, size)	Price	For self	For sale	Charge

**figure 28
example of
work schedule**

WORK SCHEDULE   Month_____

Name	1	2	3	4	5	6	7	8	9	10	11	12	13	14

**figure 29
example of party form**

_____PARTY

Month _____ Day_____ Year_____

Staff and volunteers

_____ _____ _____
_____ _____ _____
_____ _____ _____

Special announcements

_____ _____ _____

Refreshments (Dietary food requisitions, supplies, and so on)

_____ _____ _____
_____ _____ _____

Decorations   **Materials**

_____ _____
_____ _____
_____ _____

Entertainment

_____
_____
_____

Games and description

_____
_____
_____

Program plan of activities

Activity schedule   Staff   Prizes

_____ _____ _____
_____ _____ _____
_____ _____ _____

Room arrangement_____

_____

Birthday cards (If birthday party, list names and dates.)

_____
_____
_____

Assignments

Order refreshments: _____   Decorations: _____

Pick up refreshments: _____   Prizes: _____

Serve refreshments: _____   Entertainment: _____

Birthday cards: _____   Games: _____

Verses for cards: _____   Announcements: _____

Corsages and boutonnieres: _____ Cleanup: _____

**figure 30
example of
purchase requisition**

PURCHASE REQUISITION

Ordered from——————————————   Date wanted——————————

Ordered by—————————————   Time wanted——————————

Quantity/unit	Item	Unit price	Total cost

Authorized signature——————————————————————

chapter 3
Administration

Communication

Communication is the process by which thoughts and ideas are expressed. When a new project is initiated, often with new personnel in a new setting, adequate communication is essential if the project is to progress with a minimum of trouble and misunderstanding. In an activity program, communication must be established with many persons and departments: the administrator; the departments of nursing, physical therapy, and other services; the staff in the activity department; volunteers; residents; families of residents; and various resources in the community. Failure to develop or maintain adequate communication leads to resident dissatisfaction, family distrust, and staff unrest. When things do go wrong, it is frequently expedient to solve the problem by considering how to improve the communication between various problematic elements.

English words, of course, can have more than one meaning. Care must be taken that the words used actually communicate the ideas originally intended. Conn emphasizes the importance of effective communication and offers these guidelines for improving personal communication:

1. Crystallize your own ideas before trying to communicate to others.
2. Be careful of hidden messages such as your facial expression, tone of voice, and gestures.
3. Whenever you speak, use simple, plain words rather than long, complicated ones.
4. Use short sentences rather than long rambling collections of "ands" and "buts" that are monotonous and often difficult to follow.
5. Always speak slowly and clearly.
6. Present only one point at a time—completely.
7. Determine the objectives of your communication; every communication should have a purpose.
8. Tell your listener how he can benefit from your words, and he will pay close attention.

9. To be a good communicator, be a good listener.
10. When you are speaking in a small group, classroom, or person-to-person situation, check constantly to see how well your message is reaching your audience.[1]

If the activity director is to accomplish his purposes, he must develop and use effective communicative skills. It is not always easy to develop good public relations programs, employee relations programs, and the like. This takes time, effort, and skill. The activity director must know how to develop these communications systems and what techniques to use to produce the desired results.

Relationship with Administrator

Without the cooperation and understanding of the administration, the activity director will not be able to do the job he wants to do. The activity director must be able to communicate with his superiors in order to receive a satisfactory budget, to establish workable policies, to suggest implementation of future plans, and to do numerous things that are beneficial to residents.

The activity director should constantly communicate to the administrator the merits of the activity program by relating the nature of the planned activities to the total image and success of the institution. Holding frequent individual and group conferences with the administration, forwarding copies of the written evaluation reports of specific activities, and so forth are useful in keeping the administration abreast of the activity program. It is useful to have at least some of these conferences in the physical location where activities take place. It then becomes easier to focus upon the needs and problems of the program and to secure the administrator's involvement and acceptance of the goals of the program.

Interdepartmental Relationships

Effective operation of a successful activity program requires the maintenance of good relations and communication with other departments—and not just department heads, but the total staff. For example, the cooperation and the support of the nursing department are needed to encourage and motivate residents to attend activities and to escort residents to the activities. Sister Joel Marie and

Sister Mary Alice indicate that an activity program suffers if there is not total cooperation and coordination with nursing service.[2] The dietary department is needed for refreshments, for borrowing kitchen items, and maybe even for the use of the dining area. The housekeeping department is needed to keep the areas attractive and clean, and the maintenance department to keep equipment and furniture in the areas functional. Communication is needed with all the programs of the institution; every department or service is an important and valuable resource. *The personnel of all departments must cooperatively provide the total care program needed by residents.*

Although it is sometimes difficult, the activity director nevertheless must continually work toward cooperation with other departments. Cooperation is, of course, a two-way street. It must be recognized that other departments have their own unique problems and requirements, and therefore each must give as well as take.

In addition to the many opportunities for informal day-to-day contacts, there are several formal approaches. Among these are such programs as: orientation of all new employees to all departments, in-service education classes relating to the nature of work performed in other departments, department head meetings, employee clubs, and staff development classes crossing departmental lines.

The activity director should demonstrate to other departments that he is aware of their importance and that he respects their members as individuals. He should recognize them for a job well done and thank them when they do something for the activity program. He should ask them how the activity department can make *their* work easier or more effective. Involving others at every opportunity so that they are a part of the activity program will pay off.

Intradepartmental Relationships

Staff members within the same department must work together to serve the residents. Petty disagreements, arguments, and selfishness, if allowed to go unchecked, are harmful to the program. Staff members must supplement one another, work together, and build together. A well-formulated set of policies can be a very useful tool in bringing

[1]Conn, R. H. The art of communication. *Adult Leadership.* 17:269, Dec. 1968.

[2]Joel Marie, Sister, and Mary Alice, Sister. Nursing service: key to a successful activity program. *Geriatric Nursing.* 4:6, Aug. 1968.

about understanding and cooperation. The activity director should be fair with staff members, treat them equally, and yet know them well enough to use different techniques to encourage or discourage them in certain areas.

The director should recognize staff for what they do, compliment them for a job well done, and be willing to share the credit for successful programs with staff members who have shared the work. He should provide guidance and direction, allow the staff members to be creative, consider their suggestions, be aware of their needs, and support them. And when things have gone wrong, he shouldn't pass the buck.

An activity staff that works together as a team can enjoy its work and contribute to a successful program.

Relationships with Volunteers

Volunteers serve a very valuable function, and good communication with them is tremendously important. Positive relationships with volunteers should be developed from the time of recruiting through the interviewing and training phases, as well as when they are on the job. Volunteers are not to be coddled, but they do deserve thoughtful consideration. They should know their responsibilities and should be capable of carrying them out.

A climate of "belonging" should be established for the volunteers. They should be thoroughly familiarized with the purposes and activities of the program and permitted to make suggestions, comments, or complaints. Like everyone else in the setting, the volunteers interpret the total program to the community. Therefore, it is of prime importance that volunteer workers understand as much about the total care program as possible.

Relationships with Residents

Because the residents are those most directly affected by the activity program, an effective two-way dialog between the residents and the activity staff becomes an essential aspect of program planning. In addition to telling residents of programs planned for them, the activity staff must listen to them and try to understand their needs. Additional programs can then be modified so as to better enable residents to continue "normal living."

Residents are adults. Some may be ill, some handicapped, others confused or senile, but they are still adults. Like other adults, residents enjoy conversation—meaningful adult conversation. Program activities provide many opportunities for staff-resident conversation. This communication is necessary to motivate residents to continue participation in life, because residents, too, want to be "in on things." Residents must be a part of what is happening if the program is to be effective.

Among the more formal arrangements, the formation of a residents' council or of residents' committees provides a source for good communication. House organs or calendars of events can keep residents up to date. Posters, information on bulletin boards, public address announcements, and flyers can be used to publicize events. However, individual contact with residents remains the most successful method of encouraging participation.

When a resident is introduced to the activity program, it is important for a staff member to visit with him in order to learn about his interests, skills, and background. An appropriate choice of activity is guided in this way.

The choice of activity for a person with a physical or emotional disability may require more direction on the part of the activity leader. For the physically handicapped, the leader may need to evaluate the extent of the handicap: Does he have full range of arm motion? Can he grasp large/small objects? How is his finger dexterity/coordination? Does he have a visual problem?

In talking to the person about his abilities and giving some thought to them, the leader is able to help choose a project or activity the person is capable of doing. Often, this first success is vital to his continued participation.

If the leader has knowledge of the resident's physical therapy program, for example, he may suggest an activity that gives additional exercise and strengthening to weak muscles. Thus, a specific activity may be chosen to improve a physical (or mental) condition.

There are no rigid rules in choosing an activity for the person with a background of mental-emotional disturbance. Such a resident usually does not suffer from an acute disability that requires close medical supervision, but he has a history of illness and recovery or suffers from an illness of a nonsevere nature.

A basic guideline is to become acquainted with the individual. His interests, likes, and dislikes will become evident. Unless specific direction has come from the physician, the individual usually will choose an activity that he enjoys and that is beneficial. If undesired behavior develops, a switch to a different project is in order. Over time, it becomes evident if a person does well on work that is tedious, gross, short-term, long-term, creative, precise, or whatever and if he is able to express himself comfortably in the activity.

Relationships with Residents' Families

All too frequently, the families of residents are not actively involved in residents' activities. It must be remembered that the staff is not the resident's family and should not try to take its place. There are, however, many opportunities for the family to be included. In addition to regular visiting, the family should be encouraged to periodically have meals with the resident and to attend recreational events and worship services with him. Also, the family should be invited to attend birthday celebrations given in honor of the resident, attend planned group outings, and arrange personal family trips.

The family can often successfully encourage resident participation when the activity staff cannot. Through newsletters or other media, the family should be kept informed of activities planned. Family members should be encouraged to actively participate in programs. Examples of such participation include: showing slides, giving a talk, displaying items at an exhibit, helping on a committee, modeling in a fashion show, or presenting musical or dramatic performances. Grandchildren can also be involved. Orientation meetings, periodic general meetings, or individual conferences are often valuable in helping the family understand both its role and the role of the staff.

Public Relations

The activity director who develops good communication with the public can provide residents with programs that otherwise would not be possible. The better the public relations, the better the quality of individuals and groups, that is, performers, lecturers, hobbyists, and quiz guests, who voluntarily serve the residents. To accomplish this, the activity director should know what is going on in the community and who the leaders are. This information facilitates the contacting of appropriate persons when a program of a specific type is desired.

Sister Mary Lauriece says that the community must feel the influence of the home as a member of its team and the home must feel the influence of the community to further advance the opportunities for the aged who live there.[3]

Public Information

Public information items presented through the various news media can keep the community aware of the activities of the nursing home and give the public a favorable opinion of it. Newspapers, radio, and television are often interested when events are planned that are unique and of human interest.

A news release (figure 31, page 47) for publication or broadcast is a useful device for publicizing a program.

Planning and Scheduling

Surveying Community Resources

A list (figure 32, page 48) of clubs and organizations within the community should be developed. Temporarily, at least, the clubs and organizations should be placed in categories such as audiovisual presentations, dance, dramatics, entertainment and variety, lectures and demonstrations, music, nature, sports, worship services, and so forth. Later a list could be made of various places of interest in the community that could be considered for resident outings.

This list could also include persons that the activity staff knows or has heard of who might be considered as potential guests. Many possible contacts are suggested in chapter 6, "Life Activities."

Making Initial Contact

Prospective guests can be contacted directly or reached by telephone or letter (figure 33, page 48). The proper method of contact depends on the circumstances; most often a telephone call is adequate. The person should be contacted approximately two weeks to a month in advance of the time the program is scheduled. The activity director should give his name and title and the name of the facility. He should briefly describe the program and its purpose and then invite this person to appear on the selected date. It is wise to be prepared with one or two alternative dates in case the

[3]Lauriece, Sister M., O.S.F. Here's how you can develop a good activity program. *Professional Nursing Home*. 7:49, May 1965.

preferred date is unacceptable. If the person accepts the invitation, additional information should be given, including the time and place of the program, location of the facility, parking arrangements, and other pertinent information. The person should be thanked and told that a letter (figure 34, page 49) confirming the arrangements will be sent.

The activity director should anticipate the arrival of the guest and show him every courtesy. The director should display interest by being present and attentive during the program. Following the program, he should express appreciation for the activity on behalf of the nursing home. Within a few days he should write a thank you note or letter (figure 35, page 50) to the guest.

There are a number of advantages to such an approach. First, the program is likely to materialize; second, important persons in the community are kept close to the residents; and third, the guest, by receiving an orientation to the nursing home, can become a goodwill emissary who will be talking about the nursing home and its program with friends, relatives, and co-workers. It is likely the person will return when invited back and, in addition, may refer other programs to the nursing home.

Developing a Permanent Contact File System

After an affirmative reply from an individual or group has been received, certain basic information should be put on an index card (figure 36, page 50). This provides a ready reference for immediate follow-up (confirmation and thank you letters) and future recontact. The following information should be put on the card: the name of the person or group (if a group, the name of the person to contact), address, telephone number, how the person or group was referred, and any pertinent remarks.

By keeping a record of individuals, groups, and organizations providing services, such as the library providing films, a complete file of contacts is readily available.

Handling Referrals and New Contacts

As referrals are made by staff, volunteers, residents, families of residents, and guests, new cards can be added to the file. Also, newspapers should be checked carefully for contacts. From time to time individuals and groups receive television or radio publicity that alerts the activity director to additional new sources.

The entire procedure is a never-ending responsibility for the activity director.

Motivation

Motivating residents to participate voluntarily in activities that are intended to be enjoyable, meaningful, and beneficial is one of the most difficult challenges that an activity director faces. For purposes of discussion, three terms need to be defined: motivation, remotivation, and self-motivation.[4]

Motivation: That which excites action—verbally, physically, emotionally, mentally. It is a reason for "doing." There is motivation for everything a person does. He is prompted to react to certain things more obviously than others. He is aware of why and how he reacts to hunger, cold, heat, rain, and so forth. But he is not aware of many sources of stimuli, and actually suppresses some. There are many reasons why a person does not react to certain repressed desires. One of the most tragic is the feeling of "what's the use?" This is when remotivation is needed.

Remotivation: The restoring of that which causes action, but has been dormant or willfully repressed for some reason. This is affected by internal and external stimuli. Sometimes remotivation is effected from within. Some causes are emotional change, boredom, physical health change, environmental change, and financial change. Even here the person often is reacting to external experiences. Another method of remotivation is the "predetermined external influence" such as that instigated by the activity leader, social worker, or doctor. This means that a person in a position of leadership or authority "predetermines" to use certain techniques to stimulate specific persons toward self-motivation.

Self-motivation: The process of a person's being remotivated without his knowing a change is taking place. This is one of the goals of activities. Another goal is to stimulate the spirit of "wanting to do."

Why are some residents motivated to take a strong role in the activity program whereas others

---

[4]Definitions prepared by Richard Stracke, recreation consultant, Swope Ridge Health Care Center.

appear to have little incentive or interest? Maslow describes five levels of needs: first, *physiological needs*, such as to avoid hunger and thirst; second, *safety or security needs*, which produce a freedom from fear; third, *belongingness needs*, which encompass the areas of affection and love manifested in all humans and, in fact, are the reason people join clubs, groups, and so on; fourth, *esteem needs*, which come from wanting esteem from others as self-esteem; fifth, *self-actualization needs*, such as feeling a sense of contribution or of self-fulfillment or of being creative.[5]

Maslow's theory that all humans are motivated to the next unfulfilled need appears worthy of consideration. According to his "hierarchy of need" theory, it is possible that the basic needs of a resident have not been satisfied at a time when he is being encouraged to participate in an activity designed to fulfill a need at a higher level (and a reduced motivation impact).

For example, a patient who has suffered a recent severe cardiovascular accident enters the nursing home. This patient at first requires the utmost nursing care plus other prescribed therapeutic services. The patient would be not only unable but also uninterested in other activities, because of the importance of the pressing medical problems being encountered. After intensive rehabilitative treatment, he may progress to the level where his physiological needs are being reasonably satisfied. He may then begin making adjustments to the disability. At this time, the activity leader should begin remotivating the patient to participate in meaningful activities within the range of his capabilities. But not until this time will he have an interest, or be stimulated to become interested, in such activities as recreation.

What, specifically, can the activity director do to motivate a resident? This is a difficult question, because different people are motivated by different things and in different ways. However, some general suggestions are offered below:

- At the earliest possible point after the resident is admitted, the activity director should visit him, welcome him to the facility and try to get acquainted, ask if there is anything that the staff can do for him, briefly explain the program, and invite him to visit the activity area at his convenience. The director should say that he looks forward to seeing him again soon.
- If the new resident does not visit the area or attend an activity within the next day or two, the activity director should pay him another visit and invite him to see the activity area or room. When the first visit to the activity area is made, he should be introduced individually to other staff members, volunteers, and residents; shown some of the projects being worked on by other residents; and told about other activities that are available.
- During the first week, a staff member or volunteer should visit the resident for the purpose of learning of his background and interests through the use of an interest questionnaire (see figure 11, page 22). The staff should then review the completed questionnaire and consider activities that will be of interest to him.
- The activity director or a staff member should correct any situation that can be controlled and that is important to the involvement of the resident, such as helping with appearance or grooming; devising any aids that are necessary in order for him to participate; or providing assistance, if necessary, to reach the activity.
- The activity director should point out activities that have a direct meaning or importance to the resident and toward which he can personally relate and find satisfaction.
- The activity director should be positive in his invitation to a program, such as "I've come to walk with you to the program," rather than "Would you like to go to the program?"
- The resident should be involved in the selection, planning, and directing of activities of interest to him, when and if possible.
- The "help me" or "help others" approach will succeed in motivating some residents. Another approach is to offer a problem and allow the resident to become involved in working out the solution.
- If the resident is not self-motivated to take part in the program, the activity director might request the doctor, nurse, social worker, family, or others to encourage him.
- In some instances it may be possible and desirable to use a system of rewards for encouraging involvement or modifying behavior.

[5]Maslow, A. H. *Motivation and Personality.* 2nd ed. New York City: Harper and Row, 1970.

- In rare instances, it may be desirable to take a negative or challenging approach to stimulate the resident, such as "That's probably too detailed for you to see."

The above techniques can be used to motivate residents on an individual basis to enter into the activities. It has been said that people do not resist change; they resist the methods of change. When one method doesn't work, another should be used.

The following six steps represent a technique helpful in encouraging self-motivation during small group activities in which residents are directly engaged.[6] The technique is geared to various diagnostic groups in the broad spectrum of recreation.

- Step 1, Initial Acceptance
Establishing an atmosphere of acceptance amounts to little more than the common courtesies one would bestow upon a group of guests invited into one's own home. The activity director or other leader should personally greet each individual through vocal and physical contact (hand shake, pat on the back, and so forth). The leader should introduce himself to new members and introduce the residents to each other. The leader should keep the conversation going until all of the group are assembled and should make sure that each resident has a comfortable vantage point in the group arrangement. These considerations are important even though the leader may have seen or been with some of the residents only a few minutes before in some other area, because a special group and a time slot are being set aside for uniting in a specific important experience and event.

- Step 2, Curiosity
To initially introduce an activity, the leader can create curiosity among the residents by avoiding immediate group participation. The leader can provide introductory stimulation by showing objects used in the activity and initiating conversation about them. He can use a question such as "Does anyone know what this is?" Regardless of the item, a con-

versation can proceed with the help of the leader. A few suggestions for leading questions are: What is it used for? Has anyone here ever used it? How is it used? Each is as rich in potential conversation as the leader is capable of stimulating. After the curiosity phase has been established, it might be appropriate for the leader to assume the position of lecturer. Remembering that attention spans vary, the leader can gauge appropriate times to "move on." He should keep the activity simple and keep it moving. He should first present interesting facts about the activity, through a brief history or demonstration, and then initiate group participation as the situation warrants. It is even possible that the group might never get into the activity itself as a result of good verbal response about the activity. This can be good, for there is a next time. The leader shouldn't "milk" the group for conversation, but at the same time he shouldn't hurry through. If most of the group enjoys talking about the activity, they should be encouraged to talk. There will be some who will become irritated because of the inactivity— that is a beginning in self-motivation. Such persons will be motivated to criticize, to try to push for action. Eventually the group will be ready to act, even if it's walking out, and this is not bad—it's self-motivation.

- Step 3, Sharing
Assuming that the "talking" stage ends within a given time period, the leader must be aware that when a group gets together for a specific purpose, the degree of participation will vary. Like guests in one's home, some will go along with an activity just to be polite and considerate of others. Some, unlike guests in one's home, will overtly oppose the activity with various signs. The leader should observe and be aware of these verbal and nonverbal indications of lack of interest. Assuming they are not physical in cause, he should explore the signals. For example: "Mrs. Jones, you don't seem to be as interested in what we're doing as everyone else. Is there a reason you don't like this?" Mrs. Jones will probably tell her reason, and, whether it's realistic or not, the leader should respect her feelings and say, "We see your point, Mrs. Jones, but maybe you will bear with the rest of us while we

[6]The steps, developed by Richard Stracke, recreation consultant, Swope Ridge, are based partly on previous work on remotivation by Dorothy Haskins Smith. See *Remotivation Technique: A Manual for Use in Nursing Homes.* Philadelphia: Smith Kline & French Laboratories, Remotivation Project, 1957.

enjoy what we're doing." Mrs. Jones will probably be puzzled by this approach and pay closer attention, which may lead to participation. Again, she may leave. If she does, the leader should let her go. Then he must follow up later with a discussion with Mrs. Jones and find out why she doesn't want to share the experience with others, even though she is not personally interested. If the leader has established the climate of acceptance, each resident will have placed himself in a position of group responsibility and, with appropriate handling, will become more tolerant of the activity and group. Everyone shares experiences in the activity regardless of the degree of participation. Even the "standoff" will expose himself to some degree. The specific activity is not as important as creating this climate of sharing experiences. Tactics for different activities will vary depending upon capabilities, tolerances, and so on, but sharing should occur in any group activity. The leader should continually encourage participation by asking residents to share opinions and experiences.

- Step 4, Fun
People want fun. The leader should keep in mind that if the activity is not enjoyable in some way, the residents will have no part of it. However, the leader should be aware of the different points within an activity where "having fun" begins. For some, it's immediately; for others, it's halfway through the session; for others, it's near the end. For even others, it may be the next day before they realize they enjoyed the activity. And some will never admit having fun. A good leader knows how to gauge enjoyment and follows up with the various people in regard to the point of origin of their "having fun." If someone leaves an activity with obvious dislike, the leader should see him later and give him a chance to comfortably admit that "maybe" he did have a little fun. During the activity proper the goal is to promote enjoyment. The leader should explore with the group why some enjoy it and others don't. He should be careful to be not too analytical; rather, he should assume each person will have some element of enjoyment, even if it's only from being unable to enjoy himself.

- Step 5, Appreciation
This step is designed to prompt the resident to be aware of how he has participated. Each must be complimented in some way, for each has in some way contributed to the success of each activity. If the group spends a few minutes talking about how various people enjoyed the activity, the leader can easily set the stage for the final step.

- Step 6, Final Acceptance
This step is used for the leader to thank the group for coming. Again, somewhat like treating guests in one's home, the leader should bid each a "thank you" and a "good-bye." Each should be thanked for some specific involvement. Equally important is the "thank you" to those who contributed just through their presence and/or attention.

It must be remembered that approaches are different. The approaches the leader takes must be developed by experimenting and using those with which he feels most comfortable. Always open to new ideas and efforts, the leader also should avoid being clinical. He must rely upon his "third ear" to hear what's happening, his "third eye" to see what's happening, and his "second heart" to feel what's happening. If he can share that much of himself, the residents will enjoy themselves and look forward to the next group activity.

Motivating residents to voluntarily participate is not easy. It requires a great amount of time and effort, and at times it may seem like an overwhelming responsibility—this is the activity director's assignment.

**figure 31
example of
news release**

NAME AND ADDRESS OF ORGANIZATION

FOR IMMEDIATE RELEASE

Contact: (name, phone number)   (Date)

NURSING HOME PLANS SENIOR OLYMPICS

MORNINGSIDE—Some 100 old-timers are sure to be reaching for the liniment Thursday evening, Oct. 22. They plan to participate all day in Morningside's first Senior Olympics.

Track and field events will take place at Community Nursing Home, 5227 Fairfax Ave. All activities will be scaled to the physical limitations of residents of the home. Their average age is 80.

The senior games will begin at 10 a.m., following the lighting of the "Olympics Torch." A relay of three residents will carry the flame through the corridors of the nursing home, to Morningside's auditorium, the scene of most events.

In the auditorium, Mrs. Harold Kohler, president of the Residents' Council at the home, will light the torch. Oliver Chapman, Frieda Larsen, and Mrs. Henry Berger will be the flame carriers.

The opening event will be a volleyball game with a dozen oldsters in wheelchairs spiritedly battling a balloon over a net. Then comes a series of races: the "Mexican hop," in which a group of residents propel themselves between parallel bars; a race between persons who move with the aid of a "walker" frame; and a wheelchair relay.

Morning events will conclude with senior citizens kicking a ball for distance, putting the shot (using a cloth ball instead of a metal one), lifting weights, and cycling on a stationary exercise bike.

Bedfast patients can compete, too. They will be asked to recite favorite rhymes or bits of poetry. Judges will move from room to room to rate the recitations.

After lunch, competition will center on the discus and javelin throw (paper plates and cardboard spears being substituted for the real thing), a dart throw, a jacks contest, and a "horse and buggy" race with employees towing residents in their wheelchairs.

Awards will be presented by Clarence Johnson, administrator of Community Nursing Home, at a special ceremony Friday afternoon, Oct. 23, at 2:30.

Gold, silver, and bronze medals—made by residents in their crafts shop—will be presented to olympians who place first, second, and third, respectively, in various events.

Nowell Henderson, director of diversional activities at Community, developed the Senior Olympics, in cooperation with other staff members and volunteers. Mrs. Eldon Fitch, nursing director, and Ellen Thompson, physical therapist, were Mr. Henderson's principal assistants.

**figure 32
example of
list of
community resources**

Name of Organization	Address	Phone
Audiovisual (films and slides)		
Public library	100 First St.	333-6210
Modern Talking Pictures	211 Main St.	333-1934
Bell Telephone	940 Pine St.	333-8271
Armchair Travelers (slides)	410 Washington St.	333-3652
Dance		
Sally's Dance Studio (dance students)	921 Pine St.	333-1141
International Folk Dance Association	1134 Jackson Blvd.	333-6200
Anytown Squares (square dancers)	988 Chestnut St.	333-9672
Smith's School of Ballroom Dancing	412 Oak St.	333-4220
Dramatics		
Little Theater	2960 Circle Dr.	333-1111

**figure 33
example of
letter of request**

(Date)

Mr. James Field, Ticket Manager
P.O. Box 981
(City, State, Zip code)

Dear Mr. Field:

The purpose of my letter is to ask if you could consider allowing complimentary admission to a (name of team) game for a small group of residents from Riverside Home for the Aged.

We have been attempting to expand the recreation program offered our residents for the purpose of stimulating them to participate in normal living activities. Several residents have indicated interest in attending sports activities but we have no funds available for planning events in the community. Trips to the art gallery and garden center have attracted considerable interest, and I know a (name of sport) game would be a highlight for our senior sports fans.

If such a request is possible, I would like to suggest either September 4 or September 11. Should these dates be unacceptable we would be happy to consider another more convenient time. I would anticipate that 15 complimentary admissions would be adequate to cover the number of residents and necessary supervisory personnel. The majority of residents would be in wheelchairs, so we would be unable to climb stairs.

Thank you for your consideration. I look forward to hearing from you at your earliest convenience. I can be reached at 234-2990.

Sincerely,

Joan Cassel
Activities Coordinator

**figure 34
example of
confirmation letter**

(Date)

Mr. Lewis Brown, Director
Bagpipers—Pipe and Drum Band
814 Holly Hill
(City, State, Zip code)

Dear Mr. Brown:

We are elated that you accepted our invitation to appear as a guest on our
"What's My Line?" quiz show here at Rosewood Convalescent Center.
As stated in our recent telephone conversation, the program will begin
at 7 p.m. on (day, date), so we ask that you arrive by 6:45 p.m., if possible.
At that time I can share our program plans and go over any last-minute details
with you. In all, there will be five guests who will attempt to stump our
panel of residents.

Rosewood is a professional nursing home for the aged, chronically ill, and
infirm. We are located at 2400 Douglas Avenue. Parking facilities are available
near the north side of the building. I suggest that when you arrive you come
directly to the Information Desk, where you will be met by a volunteer
and escorted to our lounge. You may feel free to bring a guest with you.

If you have any further questions, please call me at 363-4290, extension 444.

We appreciate your cooperation and look forward to an interesting and
enjoyable evening for our residents.

Sincerely,

Jack Miller
Activities Director

**figure 35
example of
thank you note**

(Date)

Mr. John Smith, Band Director
Central High School
110 Main Street
(City, State, Zip code)

Dear Mr. Smith:

On behalf of the residents at Sunny View Nursing Home, I want to thank you and your band for the fine musical performance last Friday evening, May 24. The outdoor concert was considered very successful and received numerous complimentary remarks from residents, many of whom were at first apprehensive about going outside of the building. It may interest you to know that a total of 60 residents attended the program, one of our highest marks for an evening program.

Please express our thanks to each of the band members. We will look forward to next year in the hope that you can provide a return visit.

Sincerely,

Robert Jones
Director of Activities

**figure 36
example of
contact card**

Brown, Mr. and Mrs. Robert   333-4145   SLIDES
3414 E. Rosewood
(City, State, Zip code)

Slides of England, France, and Germany
Can provide a general selection or limit to one country.
Referred by John Smith.

Comments: need electrical outlet, have their own projector and screen— limit to 45 minutes. Mr. Brown uses a pointer; Mrs. Brown gives narration.

chapter 4
Therapeutic Specialties

The purpose of this chapter is to briefly describe how various therapeutic specialties relate to the activity program, point out the boundaries of these specialty professions, describe how the methods of specialists can be incorporated into a broader program, and suggest how the services of consultants can be secured and utilized.

The principal specialties referred to are institutional chaplaincy, occupational therapy, and recreational therapy. These are highly developed specialties whose philosophies, principles, techniques, and tools went into creating the activity program on which this manual is based. Some techniques from physical therapy and speech therapy were also applied. Art therapy, bibliotherapy, industrial therapy, and music therapy are other specialties that, although not specifically identified as such, were incorporated into the total program.

Professionals working in these specialties can be of great value to the activity director by integrating all these specialties into the program.

The term *therapy*, which is used considerably in this chapter, is defined as the influence that brings about specific change and the process by which an individual is modified physically and/or emotionally.

The therapies have a common goal of aiding the rehabilitation of persons with physical and emotional disabilities. Each field specializes to some degree within this broad goal. In working with elderly persons, it is helpful to view rehabilitation as restoration of health to the highest possible level, with due consideration of individual limitations. Further, maintenance of health at its present level is also a part of rehabilitation. This is often the goal—and an important one—in programs for the elderly.

Institutional Chaplaincy

The institutional chaplain is normally a fully ordained minister serving on the staff full time or part time. His qualifications include denominational requirements for ordination as well as the necessary clinical training, with emphasis on geriatrics to qualify him as an institutional specialist. His function is primarily in the counseling and relating areas, both formally and informally, and in dealing with problems of a spiritual, personal, or emotional nature. His attitude should be one of understanding and openness to the personal needs of patients, as well as to the frustrations and needs of the staff who serve at the institution. His basic concerns are human concerns and human helpfulness. His goal is to aid in leading into the fuller life, and thus in promoting a life-therapy process for those who must cope with handicaps and frustration. His resources include all of his particular religious tradition, plus a thorough grasp of the human condition and the qualities of personal identity and development.

Those who deal with the healing and life therapies have become aware of both the complication of the process and the need for the many specialties to be applied cooperatively. Thus, the team concept of therapy has developed as the various specialists have become more appreciative of each other's skills. Illness and aging are more than organic or physical processes; they involve matters of attitude, mood, and personal evaluation. Any specialty that contributes positively is part of the restoring and growth process, and the omission of any of the approaches can limit the growth of the total person.

A good institutional chaplain does not usurp another's field. Rather, he respects the capabilities and methods of each of the disciplines. In turn, he offers his own approach as a contribution to the total therapy, feeling no professional jealousy but adding his own training and abilities to the therapeutic team.

The principles of institutional chaplaincy can be incorporated into the total program even when such a resource specialty is not available or not feasible. Theological formulas and answers are seldom called for in religious counseling, but rather a patient presence and understanding as the resident seeks to work through his own spiritual needs, affirming both his faith and his doubts. The process involves such talents as the ability to listen and to convey to another person the feeling of understanding, the acceptance of each person's individuality and his right to be himself, rather than to fit a formal religious pattern or belief.

Dealing with patients as adult and mature individuals, accepting them as important in their own right, and expecting that they, in turn, will accept others in the same manner are basics of the chaplaincy. These basics often take considerable training, personal experience, and skill; they cannot be applied automatically. The matter of full respect and expectation of each other as human beings can easily be incorporated in all specialties and programs.

There are at least three ways to find a religious consultant. One way is to contact a chaplain already established in a local institution. If he cannot serve, he may be able to recommend a qualified person. Another way is to contact denominational leaders who have background and experience records on local pastors. A third way is to consult with the other specialists or with physicians who may have had unusually good relationships with a particular minister and who have observed him in his work. Their recommendation would be particularly helpful in establishing the team concept of therapy.

Occupational Therapy

Occupational therapy utilizes purposeful activity as treatment in helping a person achieve rehabilitation. The more common activities utilized are:

- Activities of daily living (ADL)—eating, dressing, bathing, writing, and so forth. These activities employ devices and adaptations of the environment to facilitate the personal skills of those with physical handicaps.
- Arts and crafts, hobbies, special interests, avocations.
- Prevocational tasks and testing. Vocational activities in geriatrics are limited, but should not be discounted. Homemaking tasks are an example of one vocational area that can be developed.

An occupational therapy (OT) program is initiated through: (1) individual medical referral (the patient's physician writes orders for OT, as he would for other medical treatment) and (2) "blanket" medical referral (some medical institutions, and often geriatric facilities, include OT services for all their clients). The program may include specific plans and treatment for individuals as well as activities that encourage group participation and socialization. A registered occupational therapist should be in charge of the occupational therapy program at all times.

The activity assistant or aide can be trained in many areas of occupational therapy. He can be trained on the job or can become a certified occupational therapy assistant through a course offered by the American Occupational Therapy Association. As the aide gains experience, he becomes capable in more technical areas of treatment. Treatment utilizing highly technical theory would, in most cases, be carried out by the therapist. However, knowledge of the theory of occupational therapy utilized in an activity department can help the staff meet patients' needs for physical and emotional restoration.

The activity department takes part in the rehabilitation program in numerous ways. Residents should be encouraged to do things for themselves whenever possible. In any activity, the physical and mental capacities of individuals should be stimulated, challenged, and utilized. This helps to maintain and increase the resident's capacity to function. The resident's self-esteem and self-image often are closely related to the abilities he believes he has. The elderly person, often given to complaining, enlists sympathy and assistance. He knows he is not the same as he was in his prime, young years. Yet he continues to need challenge, to seek the normal living that maintains the human being—body and spirit.

The Occupational Therapy Guidelines (figure 37, page 55) describe some aids and adaptations for activities of daily living.

Recreational Therapy

Among the paramedical professions contributing to the rehabilitation and maintenance of nursing home residents is recreational therapy. Early in its existence, recreational therapy was conducted mainly by those persons who had a community recreation background or persons who seemed to be otherwise best equipped to organize and direct activities in an institution. For the most part, psychiatric patients were involved in these early programs, because it was for them that physicians first recognized the therapeutic value of activities in treatment of certain emotional illnesses. It was not long after that when recreational activities were used with many groups, and even spectator and other diversional activities were accepted as therapeutic or helpful in treatment.

To discuss the differences among diversional activities, recreational activities, and recreational therapy, personal points of reference must be considered. Some would say there are few or no differences.

It might be safe to say that recreational therapy is an activity prescribed by a physician, or at least approved by a physician, for a certain patient or group of patients and is directed to accomplishing predetermined goals.

Diversional activities may be said to be the same kinds of activities set up by or for one resident or a group of residents because of the obvious need for such a program. The personal qualifications of the leader will determine to a great extent the effectiveness of the "therapy." Whatever it is called, the activity *is* therapy—either good therapy or poor therapy. In either case, some of the unconscious needs of the resident are met through manipulation of the environment.

Recreational therapy, now a recognized profession, has national standards for certification, and several colleges and universities offer degrees in this specialty. There are numerous well-qualified pioneers in this field who have neither the national certification nor the degree but who function effectively.

It is pointless to argue the degree of "therapy" produced under different leadership situations. On the other hand, it is obvious that there is a relation between the quality of therapeutic climate in a nursing home and the qualifications of the leaders.

All institutions are interested in getting the most value for the least amount of money. In selecting leadership in diversional activities or recreational therapy, an administrator must first determine his goals and then decide what is possible and hire accordingly.

Physical Therapy

Physical therapy is discussed only briefly as a restorative service, because in its normal structure it cannot be within the diversional activities program. This is not to say, however, that the physical therapy and the activity departments cannot coordinate their efforts, as each can provide assistance and support for the other's efforts.

Physical therapy utilizes technical apparatus, in part, in achieving objectives and requires the direction of a registered therapist. The purpose of physical therapy is to maintain and restore a person's health through the modalities of exercise, heat, water, light, and electricity. Such treatment can be given only under a physician's prescription. Every geriatric facility should have physical therapy, so basic is it for maintaining the elderly patient's physical strength and for rehabilitation after illness.

Speech and Hearing Services

The goal of speech therapy in a geriatric setting is redevelopment of communication skills that have been impaired as a result of injury or disease.

Speech evaluations are given by a speech pathologist or other person with proper accreditation. He directs follow-up therapy that, if the facility does not have specially trained personnel, can be administered by attendants, such as diversional activity aides and nursing aides, on a regular schedule with the resident. An occupational therapist is partially trained in methods of speech therapy and can provide assistance in this area as he helps the resident develop other skills used daily.

Because hearing problems often accompany old age, audiology is another valuable specialty to be considered in the restorative services offered. Specialists in audiology test and diagnose hearing disturbances, fit hearing aids, and often are involved in the related speech therapy.

Because most nursing homes are not large enough to require full-time employment of speech and hearing specialists, there is a growing trend to use the speech and hearing department of a nearby hospital on a consultant basis. Some departments now avail themselves of facilities and individuals outside the hospital. There is often government funding to support such services. This arrangement is ideal for the nursing home, as the consultancy is a flexible arrangement in which the consultant varies his time according to patients' needs for services.

The Speech Therapy Guidelines (figure 38, page 56) can help with the rehabilitation of an aphasic patient's speech and language skills. These suggestions are directed primarily to the nurse, for the nurse is the one who will be spending the most time with the patient. Actually, every member of the staff who has any dealings with the patient —doctor, intern, speech pathologist, psychologist, physiotherapist, occupational therapist, activity director—must cooperate in the speech and language therapy program in order that the patient can derive the maximal benefit. Later, when the family takes over the major responsibility of daily care of the patient, the members must unite their efforts in carrying out the therapeutic program.

Counseling

Individuals in the nursing or retirement home occasionally need personal counseling. The problems of illness, adjustment to living with others and with some regimentation, adjustment to the confines of older age, and settling of estates and finances are only a few problems that are encountered.

Qualified counselors are available in various fields, such as education, religion, psychology, psychiatry, and social work. The use of a counselor as the need arises provides a valuable service to the residents and to the integral functioning of the home.

In-Service Training

Continued exposure to the philosophies and methods of the specialties referred to in this chapter can be gained from participation in multidisciplinary in-service training programs.

In-service training programs contribute to the overall growth and development of all personnel. These training classes can improve and increase abilities, knowledge, attitudes, and motivations. It is obvious that staff members in all services and departments, including the activity department, will be more capable of doing their best job when they are properly trained.

In order to more effectively carry out their assignments, volunteers too should be included in the in-service programs, whether they are assisting in the activity program or are assigned to other departments.

figure 37
occupational therapy
guidelines

OCCUPATIONAL THERAPY GUIDELINES

Eating and Drinking

Eating utensils designed for a person with impaired arm/hand function include swivel spoons and forks, combination fork-spoons, extension handles, handles built up with foam rubber, and rocker knives (for a one-handed person).

Drinking aids include extended-length straws and straws bent for the individual (for those unable to hold or handle a glass or cup); straw holders, such as simple pencil clips, to secure straw to glass; glass or cup holders; and special cup handles.

A damp cloth placed under dishes keeps them from sliding. Plate guards attached to plates help the one-handed person scoop food onto utensil. Suction cups on dish bottoms hold them securely.

Dressing

Long-handled reachers/graspers are used to pick up objects by a person with limited mobility.

Elastic shoelaces eliminate tying and lacing.

Many garments are available or can be adapted for the wearing ease of the handicapped person; for example, front openings (zippers and Velcro® openings are easiest), wraparound style clothes.

Pamphlets are available showing easy steps in dressing for hemiplegic, one-handed, arthritic, and other patients.

Bathing, Toilet, and Grooming

Bars and railings are installed in bathrooms to meet specific needs. Other aids include raised toilet seat, chair or seat in tub, and nonskid tub mats.

Bathing aids include soap on string for around neck, washcloth mitt with pocket for soap, and long-handled brush.

Grooming aids include electric toothbrush, mirror on stand, mirror with hook handle around neck, magnifying mirror, cosmetic trays and holders, long-handled combs and brushes, electric razors, and special holders for razors.

Reading and Writing

Reading aids include magnifying glasses, prism glasses (for lying position), reading racks to hold or position material for the bedridden patient and others, and large-print magazines and books for the person with a visual handicap.

Special devices are available for the person who cannot hold a pen or pencil. Ball-point and felt-tip pens are best for some (felt-tip pens are easiest to see).

To stabilize paper a person can use a clipboard, paper can be taped to table, or a typewriter pad or textured surface can be placed underneath.

Typewriting may enable a person to "write." A one-handed typing method has been developed. The person can use typing sticks, if not fingers.

figure 38
speech therapy
guidelines

SPEECH THERAPY GUIDELINES

1. Be relaxed and calm around the patient. Try to keep him happy and contented with himself and his surroundings. Avoid forcing him to do things.

2. Avoid making any issue as to the patient's lack of speech. Always phrase your questions so the patient can answer with a yes or no, or nod of the head. Keep in mind that in some instances a patient indicates yes when he actually means no, and vice versa.

3. Anticipating what the patient is trying to say by voicing it for him markedly impedes progress in speech and language development. Always encourage the patient to speak and do things for himself, but never make *an issue* over his doing it. If he can read, encourage him to sign his name rather than make a cross for his signature. Let him take care of his grooming and his physical needs as much as possible. Being allowed to do things for himself helps the patient build self-respect.

4. Accept an aphasic patient *as he is*. Let him express himself freely on his own speech and language level. Exert every effort to understand what he is trying to tell you whether it be in words, distorted syllables, or pantomime.

5. If the patient swears or voices emotional utterances, *avoid any show of disapproval*. To express annoyance or reprove a patient only inhibits his attempts at communication and may cause withdrawal "into his shell." He will then avoid all efforts to speak.

6. Avoid all discussion pertaining to "before" or "after" the patient's accident, injury, stroke, or whatever, and never mention his speech inabilities.

7. Avoid putting pressure on the patient to get him to utter a complete sentence. If he says only the essential words (for example, nouns, pronouns, and action verbs), show pleasure over such speech efforts. Brief utterances made during post-traumatic days are most acceptable efforts, and they should be praised.

8. When handing the patient an object such as a fork, repeat the word *fork* several times. Say it in a confident modulated voice—never with a rising questioning inflection. Similarly, when bathing him, call the name of the part of the body several times as you wash it. At first, use words such as arm, hand, leg, foot, toe; later, use words such as back, ear, head, face, chin. Use only one-syllable words at first, then two-syllable words such as elbow and shoulder.

9. Should the patient indicate a desire to be helped with a word, pronounce it slowly and distinctly. Avoid saying "Watch me as I say it" or "Put your tongue here" or the like. Directions regarding correct use of speech musculature are handled by the therapist during the session. Most therapists will discuss and demonstrate to the attendant what can be done to help the patient, especially if he requests such assistance.

10. When the patient seems unable to say a certain word or phrase or cannot perform a given task *avoid showing concern*. Suggest that he do some-

Adapted from guidelines of Menorah Medical Center, Department of Speech and Hearing, Kansas City, MO. Original source unknown.

**figure 38
(cont.)**

thing else you feel he can do. If he indicates that he doesn't want to try another activity, help him to complete the first task. Never reprimand, scold, or tease the patient because he is unable to carry out an activity.

11. If the patient tries to tell you something and you can't understand him, suggest by word and pantomime that he draw a picture of what he is trying to say.

12. When the patient shows fatigue, suggest a change of activity or rest—depending on the degree of fatigue. However, avoid negative suggestions, such as "You're tired now; let's do something else." Avoid all references to fatigue, anxiety, or tension. Simply intersperse activity with rest periods. Avoid overstimulating the patient. Never suggest too much rest, for that may cause anxiety, withdrawal, and loss of initiative.

13. Avoid discussing with the patient problems pertaining to his family or friends or other patients in the hospital. These problems are *not* his concern. The aphasic's primary problem is himself—his handicaps and his needs.

14. Take advantage of the patient's feeling of euphoria (sense of well-being) even though he may have a serious disability. The patient's lack of concern about his condition in the early postmorbid days can be used to motivate constructive habits for speech and language therapy activities and for physical and occupational therapy. Never discuss euphoria as such with the patient, because this is his defense (by denial) against subconscious anxiety.

15. Try to meet all accidents on the part of the patient in a relaxed manner. For instance, make no issue of his spilling food on his robe or tipping over a glass of water. Always strive to establish and maintain rapport with the patient. Perhaps a comment like "Accidents do happen" accompanied by a real smile will help him to feel less ashamed in the difficult situation.

16. Never make any issue about practicing speech or writing, because suggestions for practice should come from the patient.

17. When helping the patient review material in his speech notebook, make certain that the review session ends on a successful note. Closing the practice period with an unsuccessful attempt depresses the patient and impedes progress.

18. Avoid saying "Now relax—and then you say it." (Suggestions for relaxation are often helpful for a spastic, athetoid, or polio patient but not for an aphasic person.) To tell the aphasic to relax is distracting and upsetting. You may even precipitate an anxiety or catastrophic attack. Assume a calm, friendly attitude, and avoid any show of concern or anxiety when he has difficulty in responding.

19. When helping the patient with his speech review, see that *no one* else is in the room. Extraneous stimuli are most distracting to the aphasic individual.

20. It was explained to the patient during the first therapy session that speech progress will require time and effort. It is necessary for the patient to

figure 38 (cont.)

recognize and accept these factors; otherwise, he tends to become even more discouraged about his aphasia problem. The less said about the time and effort involved, the better. Above all, avoid remarks like, "You'll be well in just a short time," because these lead to disillusionment.

21. The patient continually needs help in recognizing his major goals, his subgoals, and his day-to-day goals. These will frequently be discussed with the patient during therapy sessions. As these day-to-day goals are reached, commend his progress. Such recognition aids him in further goal setting and attainments.

22. All new words are presented in the therapy sessions. *Never* permit the patient to write a word without saying it aloud. The word must be written and spoken as one unified process.

23. Avoid all mention of spelling. That problem is resolved automatically as the patient learns to write and say the word. If he attempts to spell aloud, just suggest: "Let's say and write it."

24. Suggest various pastimes for the patient. Do this even while he is still bedridden. Suggest activities in which you are confident that the patient can be successful and participate with him in the activity. For example, if a woman patient starts a knitting project, the nurse should knit too. By continually motivating the patient to constructive, worthwhile activities, you are helping him to avoid self-destructive behavior such as withdrawal and depression.

25. Familiarize yourself with various aspects of the patient's behavior. Study them in the light of his speech and language problems. Keep in mind that the patient is *not* a "different" person because he has aphasia. He is just reacting to his environment in the light of his present difficulties.

chapter 5
Volunteer Program

The volunteer system can best be considered as a triangle consisting of the volunteer, the nursing home, and the resident. To be successful, the volunteer system must be a happy and functional blending of the interests, skills, and talents of the volunteer with the needs and requirements of the resident and with the philosophy of the nursing home. Much of its success depends upon the mutual respect and understanding that can develop among these three parts of the "triangle." Therefore, it is important that the volunteers and/or organizations that may provide volunteers thoroughly understand the policies and procedures of the nursing home and its needs for volunteer assistance. It is equally important that the staff members understand these same policies and procedures as well as those of any outside organization that might provide volunteers.

There is no way to adequately define a volunteer, because volunteers come in all shapes and sizes, from all walks of life, and from all sorts of previous training and experience. Volunteerism knows no favorite age, sex, or place. About the only things that unite volunteers into a single class are the facts that they have a strong desire to be of service and that they do not receive monetary rewards.

Volunteers, if properly used, do receive rewards. Self-satisfaction, self-esteem, and the friendships that emerge from their work usually return to the volunteers more than they give. It is the obligation of the nursing home staff and administration to ensure that conditions are maintained so that volunteers receive these rewards.

Two points need special emphasis. First, volunteer services do not substitute for the services of paid staff; rather, they supplement and complement them. It is most important that all interested parties understand this. Nothing can erode volunteer-staff relationships more quickly than

Marie Santee, director of voluntary service, Kansas City (MO) Veterans Administration Hospital, was a major contributor to this chapter.

misunderstandings over this point. The services of volunteers are of value to the home not so much because volunteers add manpower to the staff but because they provide many unique contributions that only they can make as members of the community, proving their concern for residents of the nursing home. The additional manpower provided by volunteers is frequently not large, because it takes paid staff time to orient and supervise these workers. Whether or not the volunteers add significantly to the available staff time, their contributions are still most important to the total organization, because they provide nursing home residents with new services and with an unalterable testimony that the "outside world" has not forgotten them.

Second, volunteer services are not free. Although volunteers give their services without monetary remuneration, the administration of the institution must recognize that there are expenses, both direct and indirect, in the planning, training, and supervision of volunteer work.

Volunteers are important not only by virtue of what they do but also by virtue of the fact that *they are there.* With proper guidance and training, they can contribute in valuable ways to the care and treatment of residents. Over and above the special talents and skills they bring to staff and residents, they make special contributions because they are *not* members of the staff; because they represent no particular treatment discipline; because they form a link between the nursing home and the community from which the residents have come; because they provide interpersonal relationships that are flexible within a variety of experiences; and because they represent an unhurried permissiveness, which contrasts with the more authoritative roles of staff.

Although volunteers provide a valuable service by just being present, acceptance of volunteer service must be based on specific need of the staff or the residents. This need must be communicated to the volunteers, so that assignments will have direction and purpose. Naturally, whenever possible, placement should be commensurate with the interests and skills of the workers. But the administration and the staff must not make the mistake of assuming that the volunteers will necessarily know how to apply these skills to a particular problem. Proper orientation and training are almost always necessary before the volunteers can operate at maximum efficiency.

Volunteers can be differentiated according to their basic function, as follows:

1. Direct-service volunteers are those who participate in programs with and for the residents. Direct-service workers can perform either therapeutic services or social-support services.
2. Administrative-service volunteers are those who donate their time and talents within the community in the interpretation of the program or perform other functions not directly related to resident care.

Volunteers may receive individual assignments, when they operate more or less on their own, or group assignments, when they work as a team. Volunteers may be regularly scheduled (serving according to a specific schedule) or occasionally scheduled (serving sporadically).

Specifics about the expectations from and by staff as well as from and by volunteers are covered in other sections of this chapter. However, all concerned should bear in mind that an effective volunteer program is never just one type of thing or one type of person. Diversity and flexibility are the watchwords as the volunteer program is being designed for its major purpose—to make the life of the residents more livable.

Director of Volunteers

It is the responsibility of the nursing home administration to develop and maintain the proper climate for a successful volunteer program that will be meaningful to all three elements of the volunteer system—the volunteers, the staff, and the residents.

A volunteer program will not operate itself. However, it is unrealistic to expect the regular staff to expend much energy in recruiting, training, or supervising volunteers. Therefore, these functions need to be assigned specifically to one person, the director of volunteers. For a limited activity program, the director's job should be made a part of someone else's job description. For a large program, a full-time director should be employed. In most nursing homes, the director's job is a part-time assignment. The most likely person to receive this responsibility (although others should be equally interested) is the director of activities.

In any case, the duties of the director of volunteers are to:

- Determine, in conjunction with the nursing home staff, areas in which volunteer services are needed.
- Develop and coordinate community resources to meet the nursing home's needs.
- Interpret to department heads the potentials for available volunteer services, and indicate the areas in which volunteer participation can contribute to the welfare of residents.
- Assist department heads in the preparation of guidelines for services and requests for volunteer services.
- Develop recruitment plans in the community through individual contacts and community organizations.
- Be responsible for interviewing, screening, and selecting regular volunteers.
- Arrange for basic orientation, in-service training, placement, and supervision of volunteers in various departments.
- Review with departments the performance, reassignments, or resignations of volunteers. (Exit interviews provide excellent guides for program improvement.)
- Establish a system of recording volunteer hours, to facilitate future recognition of volunteers.
- Meet at least quarterly with the advisory committees to interpret and evaluate the volunteer program, to establish plans for volunteer recognition, and to set policies regarding volunteer benefits. These will generally be separate meetings.
- Establish a system of acknowledgment, receipt, and distribution of donations.
- Keep the volunteers informed of pertinent nursing home policies and procedures.
- Keep the nursing home staff informed of the availability of services and community resources.
- Maintain a close relationship with the community, being cognizant of its resources, and aid in the interpretation of the nursing home program to the community.
- Stimulate suitable recognition of the contribution of community services to the welfare of residents.

Advisory Committees

Developing a staff advisory committee is optional, but desirable, as an advisory group can provide considerable assistance to the volunteer director. The volunteer program will benefit from having key personnel from the nursing home involved in the planning and administration of the program. This involvement is accomplished by selecting and developing a staff advisory committee, which can participate in both an advisory and an active capacity. Having a representative from the board of directors, administration, and each department that uses volunteers (preferably the department head) offers a broad perspective.

The purpose of the staff advisory committee is to assist in developing a favorable image of the nursing home program, interpreting philosophy, surveying the needs for volunteers, and making plans for meeting these needs through the use of assignment guides. The committee can also take part in developing and carrying out training programs and in evaluating and recognizing the volunteers.

Whether or not a staff advisory committee should be created depends on the size of the nursing home, the number of staff members, the size of the community, and the availability of community organizations. When conditions do not favor formation of such a committee, the need to use the principles of involvement and good communication still remains.

Community involvement in the program can be accomplished by establishing a community advisory committee, which would meet with the staff advisers. This group should be made up of responsible leaders of selected community organizations. There is really no limit to the number of organizations that can be involved, but it is suggested that only four to six organizations be involved at first. Examples of organizations that might be represented from the beginning are the American Red Cross, American Association of Retired Persons, local garden club, local music club, Boy Scouts of America, Girl Scouts of America, and National Federation of Women's Clubs. Other possibilities are the ministerial alliance, fraternal organizations, unions, sororities, and high school student councils. The committee should be composed of a representative and an alternate from each organization. Whenever possible, both should be present at the meetings, to stabilize communication at those times when one is absent.

The basic responsibility of the community advisory committee is twofold: (1) to assist in the recruitment, screening, and training of volunteers to meet the nursing home needs; and (2) to assist the staff in the interpretation of the program within the community.

At a monthly or quarterly meeting with the staff advisory committee, the community representatives can gain further insight into the nursing home program so as to properly interpret it within the community. They can interpret their own organization's policies, procedures, and plans for recruitment, screening, and placement of volunteers and can assist with plans to meet the nursing home's needs for volunteers.

Attitudes of Staff

Key persons in the success of a volunteer program are the staff members who use volunteers, as healthy attitudes on the part of these staff members help to create and develop a climate of acceptance and respect toward the volunteers. These healthy attitudes reflect the staff members' emotional maturity and security in their jobs. These individuals are not threatened by the use of volunteers, knowing full well that well-screened, well-placed, and well-trained volunteers are an extension of the hands, hearts, and minds of the staff. These staff members recognize that the essence of volunteer work is in the intangibles. They also are cognizant of the generally high caliber of volunteers and their wide gamut of talents, which are often unique.

The creative imagination of the staff is challenged by the task of putting the skills and talents of volunteers to work and thus utilizing them to their highest potential, knowing that this usually makes for the happiest volunteers. Staff members must be careful not to insult the volunteers by giving them menial jobs or busywork or letting them be idle. Volunteers must be given assignments that are meaningful.

The effectiveness of volunteers is increased by their knowing they are a part of a team. Volunteers should therefore *not* be an entity unto themselves, but should be an integrated part of the programs they serve.

All echelons of the staff, especially the first-line supervisors, must help in creating the proper cli-

mate for volunteer use. The investment of staff time and effort will pay off in happy, satisfied, and enthusiastic volunteers who will be their own best publicity agents, both inside and outside the institution.

Establishing Need

To produce an effective volunteer program, volunteer needs must first be anticipated. These needs should be defined and backed with specific written guidelines for volunteers. Also, a method of administration, training, and supervision of such a program must be established.

Department heads can be of value by considering ways in which they can use volunteers. There are no doubt many places where volunteers could be used. Many spots require no particular skills or talents other than the ability to work with different people in different settings and the ability to stimulate and encourage others. These generalists can be helpful in a variety of ways.

Consider, for example, a volunteer who works one day a week for four hours as a staff assistant to the activity program. She could assist a resident working on a project requiring some manual dexterity, being reminded to help only as much as is absolutely needed. She could go to a resident's room to encourage attendance at an activity. She could have a cup of coffee or a cold drink with a resident who is withdrawn, as a means of getting to know him better and providing needed personalized attention. She could aid a resident with a grooming problem. She could take a resident for a walk or sit and chat with him on the porch. She could pick up a library book for a resident and bring in a home-grown plant for another. She could be a hostess at a party or help on an outing. This list of possibilities is endless; the director of volunteers can suggest tasks that fit the residents of the particular nursing home.

In the beginning the volunteer will require direction and instruction, but as she becomes more comfortable and the staff gains confidence in her readiness to use more initiative, she can be granted freedom within the limits of her job description. For the volunteer who is a generalist, the qualities of caring, pleasantness, and enthusiasm are more important attributes than any particular skills.

In addition to needing the generalists, the nursing home might need volunteers who possess a special talent or ability, that is, persons with a particular background, such as art, carpentry, games, gardening, genealogy, research, music, photography, or sewing.

The Volunteer Service Assignment Guide (figure 39, page 66) is used to describe the duties and qualifications of various types of volunteers. A different assignment guide should be prepared for each volunteer position. Volunteers who are generalists include the companionship therapist and the transportation aide (figures 39a through 39m, pages 67 through 79). Volunteers who are specialists include the art instructor and the clerical aide (figures 39n through 39y, pages 80 through 91).

Another useful form for determining need for volunteers is the Request for Volunteer Service (figure 40, page 92), which is filled in by any staff member in need of volunteers.

Recruitment

To begin a volunteer program in a nursing home, the director of volunteers should first look at community sources for volunteers. They usually include churches, public and private volunteer service agencies, women's organizations, men's clubs, and youth programs.

The first seeds of thought about volunteering can be planted in several different ways. Without a doubt, direct personal contact is the best method. This can be complemented by the use of audiovisual and printed materials.

The director of volunteers can participate as a speaker at a program of a community organization. Several different approaches can be used in talking with a group about volunteering. For example, as a guest speaker, the director of volunteers could select as a topic "The Need for Volunteers in Our Nursing Home" or "The Improvements in the Quality of Care Now Being Given in Long-Term Facilities." In the latter case something should be included about how volunteers are needed now to continue this trend. Displays, photographs, or a short slide presentation illustrating how volunteers relate to residents can be valuable. The speaker should emphasize examples of an extra zest for life received by residents through relationships with volunteers.

After the program, the director of volunteers should get the names of persons who would like more information about volunteers. Then they should be sent personal notes thanking them for their special interest. They should be invited to see the nursing home and learn about its program. They should be told about the types of volunteers that are needed and why. This initial visit should lead up to the screening and orientation process, which is described in the next section of this chapter.

Another approach is for the director of volunteers and the residents to do something that is of special interest to a particular organization in the community. For instance, if the members of an organization sew dressings or other items for the cancer society, residents could sew and contribute such items to that organization. Other ideas are for residents to make homemade ice cream to send over to a club for dessert or to build kites to be given to a young people's group. Any return from these services will result in a sharing experience that will benefit all.

Recruitment can also be initiated by bringing a person or a group to the nursing home itself. This technique exposes people from the community to the nursing home's physical plant and residents. Such guests might be invited to speak at a lecture program, to exhibit something they may have to show, or to give a slide presentation, choral program, or other appropriate activity. They might be asked to give advice on a related subject. For example, a garden club might be asked about a problem the nursing home is having with flower boxes. A Bible study group might be invited to participate with residents in a discussion group. Members of a scout troop might be asked to earn service badges at the nursing home by helping with bingo, making posters, or whatever.

Once the group leaders or members have been contacted, the director of volunteers and other staff members should consider how these groups can continue to help and how they might be useful and interested in other activities that urgently need volunteers.

The director of volunteers can also:

- Visit a local voluntary action center and seek its assistance. The same can be done with the Retired Senior Volunteer Program (RSVP) and the American Red Cross.

- Offer to provide meeting space for appropriate types of organizations.

- Set up a volunteer information booth at an annual open house or at a community health fair.

- Seek advertising space or inclusion of an article in business house organs and church bulletins.
- Use public-service promotions, such as radio and television spots, ads in "shoppers," and bus and taxi signs, to recruit volunteers.
- Plan a direct-mail information program.
- Use posters in store windows or announcements on bulletin boards.
- Buy radio time or advertise in the newspaper. A 30-second spot (figure 41, page 93) and a one-minute spot (figure 42, page 93) prepared for radio could also be adapted for use as newspaper ads for the same purpose.

Screening and Orientation

Getting the right volunteer in the right assignment is the essence of good placement. Volunteers should be comfortable in their assignments. Uncovering the skills, talents, and interests of the prospective volunteer is the responsibility of the director of volunteers. The Volunteer Application Form (figure 43, page 94) and the Volunteer Interview Form (figure 44, page 95) are valuable aids in discovering these skills and interests and in gathering other important information. During an interview, information that will permit the best and wisest placement can be gained.

In selecting volunteers, special attention should be given to their attitudes toward others, toward leisure, and toward life in general. These should include their capacity and zest for living, creative attitudes, scientific attitudes, social attitudes, ability to lead democratically, and technical skills.

After the volunteers have been selected, some general orientation facts should be explained to them. To some extent the volunteers will receive orientation from recruitment information and efforts. However, in order to make sure that each volunteer is fully aware of her responsibility, an orientation program is needed. In addition to a full explanation of the philosophy that underlies the volunteer program, a number of other principles need to be covered, such as the following:

- All tasks are important whether they are simple or complex. Each job must be done well.
- No one job is more or less important than any other. Each assignment has its place in the total scheme of things.
- Each volunteer has different skills and talents to bring to the program. Every effort will be made to make maximum use of these skills for the benefit of the residents.
- It is better to underestimate than overestimate the amount of time that the volunteer can donate to the program.
- Dependability is as important in the volunteer as it is in the paid staff member. The resident must be able to count on the volunteer doing the assignment at the proper time.
- Dependability and promptness affect the quality of programs and the quality of life for the residents.
- The volunteer will receive many benefits from participation in the program. Some of the benefits may not be apparent immediately, but they are just as real and rewarding.

Training and Supervision

A good executive delegates authority and responsibility. This is important in the assignment of volunteers to their various positions. But first, volunteers must be trained for their assignments.

Not only are volunteers entitled to a basic orientation and initial training for their specific assignments, but on a periodic basis they should be brought back for continued in-service training and refresher courses. Continuing education is an investment of time and effort on the part of staff that pays high dividends in enthusiastic, knowledgeable volunteers who will be the best source of recruitment for new volunteers.

Volunteers should be trained in the following areas:

- In methods of working *with*, not *for* residents
- In knowledge of their own volunteer assignments
- In knowledge of the nursing home and its various services and programs
- In interpersonal relationships

Staff as well as volunteers should be trained in interpersonal relationships, for understanding oneself helps in better understanding of others.

Volunteers need guidance from the professional staff, both for routine communication and for periodic evaluation. Training, and keeping volunteers informed as members of the working team, will unleash an amazing drive for accomplishing goals.

Forms that are helpful in administering the program include a Volunteer Sign-In Record (figure 45, page 96) and a Volunteer Vacation Schedule (figure 46, page 97). The sign-in record is a useful tool as a control and information device and also as a record of hours for use in preparing for the volunteer appreciation ceremony.

Recognition

The gift of a volunteer's time is valuable to all. Recognition of those who give time is a way to keep interest and enthusiasm alive. Maintaining interest protects the staff's investment in time, planning, and supervision of the volunteer program. Sincere interests and enthusiasm on the part of the volunteers mean greater benefits to the nursing home patients.

Recognition also satisfies a basic need of the volunteers. The greatest recognition that volunteers can have is the feeling of being needed. Therefore, volunteers must be given jobs that are important and challenging and that offer an opportunity for growth. Acting as ambassadors of good-will in the community, satisfied and dedicated volunteers will help recruit other volunteers.

A specific program of recognition should include:

- A thank you from the director and/or immediate supervisor at the end of each day
- A system of awards, pins, emblems, or certificates presented in accordance with established standards
- Presentation of awards at a special function such as a tea, party, banquet, or other ceremony attended by administration, staff, and volunteers

Volunteers are capable of significant work in the nursing home field. A good relationship between volunteers and professional staff leads to mutual respect and the excitement of discovering what the team can accomplish. Adequate training and utilization of the volunteers' special talents can do wonders for the care and quality of life of nursing home residents.

**figure 39
example of
volunteer service
assignment guide**

VOLUNTEER SERVICE ASSIGNMENT GUIDE

Title: Using service:

Assignment needs:

Frequency:

Hours:

Duties:

Qualifications:

Training requirements:

Supervision:

Date:

**figure 39a
volunteer service
assignment guide
arts and crafts aide**

VOLUNTEER SERVICE ASSIGNMENT GUIDE

Title: Arts and crafts aide   **Using service:** Activities

Assignment needs: Two or three (initially), one per day of choice as
determined at interview.

Frequency: Weekly.

Hours: 9:30 a.m. to 2:30 p.m.

Duties: To assist staff in the hobby house activities by:

1. Instructing and assisting residents with various arts and crafts
   projects.

2. Assisting in the cleanup of projects for the day.

Qualifications: Skills and interests in arts and crafts.
Dependability.
Interest in people.
Cheerful attitude.
Creative imagination.

Training requirements: Basic orientation and in-service
training from staff.

Supervision:

Date:

figure 39b
volunteer service
assignment guide
companionship
therapist

VOLUNTEER SERVICE ASSIGNMENT GUIDE

Title: Companionship therapist   **Using service:** Activities

Assignment needs: Five (initially) for visitation referrals to individual residents in room and bedside program.

Frequency: Weekly.

Hours: Flexible as to days and hours for individual visitation, but should be half-day each week, preferably in morning.

Duties: To assist the activity staff in the remotivation program for from one to five residents by:

1. Making weekly visitations to the referred residents.
2. Establishing interpersonal relationships with the residents to assure them of individual interest and care.
3. Helping each resident regain a favorable self-image.
4. Explosing with residents their past vocational and avocational interests.
5. Developing individual diversional activities around the residents' interests, capabilities, and tolerances.
6. Nurturing a climate for guiding residents, wherever possible and advisable, into the activity program.
7. Redeveloping lost diversional activity skills.
8. Developing a sensitivity to each resident's physical and emotional needs, and sharing this information with staff for purposes of meeting these needs.

Qualifications: A reliable evaluation of self.
Sensitivity to others' needs and interests.
Empathy, as opposed to sympathy.
Ability to listen.
Creative imagination and sense of humor.
Reliability.
Knowledge of philosophy of nursing home.
Knowledge of diversional activity program.

Training Requirements: Basic orientation and in-service training from staff and consultants.

Supervision:

Date:

**figure 39c
volunteer service
assignment guide
escort aide (nursing)**

VOLUNTEER SERVICE ASSIGNMENT GUIDE

Title: Escort aide   **Using service:** Nursing

Assignment needs: Three: one for Monday and Friday, one for Wednesday,
one for Tuesday and Thursday.

Frequency: Weekly.

Hours: 10 a.m. to 3:30 p.m.

Duties: To aid in transportation of patients within home when nursing
needs assistance.

To escort residents to and from dining room at meal times.

To escort residents to and from hobby house.

Qualifications: Must be physically able to wheel chairs.
Must have cheerful disposition.

Training requirements: Basic orientation and in-service training from the using
service in the handling of wheelchairs and litters.

Supervision:

Date:

VOLUNTEER SERVICE ASSIGNMENT GUIDE

Title: Escort aide   **Using service:** Physical therapy

Assignment needs: Five: one for each of five days, Monday through Friday.

Frequency: Weekly.

Hours: 9 a.m. to 3:30 p.m.

Duties: To assist in the transportation of patients to and from physical therapy, the beauty shop, and their own rooms.

Qualifications: Must be physically strong, must not mind walking, and must enjoy people.

Training requirements: Basic orientation and training from the using service in the handling of wheelchairs and litters.

Supervision:

Date:

**figure 39e
volunteer service
assignment guide
games instructor**

VOLUNTEER SERVICE ASSIGNMENT GUIDE

Title: Games instructor　　　　　　　　**Using service:** Activities

Assignment needs: Two: one for Tuesday, one for Thursday or any two days.

Frequency: Weekly.

Hours: 1 to 4 p.m. or 1:30 to 4:30 p.m.

Duties: To promote and set up for a variety of card and game activities.

　　　　　To instruct and assist residents in these activities.

　　　　　To encourage socialization through these activities.

Qualifications: Knowledge of games, both individual and group.
　　　　　　　Interest in learning new games.
　　　　　　　Ability to lead and instruct.
　　　　　　　Ability to adapt games to tolerances of group.
　　　　　　　A kind and considerate manner.

Training requirements: Basic orientation.

Supervision:

Date:

figure 39f
volunteer service
assignment guide
hostess

VOLUNTEER SERVICE ASSIGNMENT GUIDE

Title: Hostess   **Using service:** Dietetics

Assignment needs: Seven, one for each day for lunch.
Seven, one for each day for dinner.

Frequency: Weekly.

Hours: Lunch hours: 12 noon to 1:15 p.m.
Dinner hours: 5 p.m. to 6:30 p.m.

Duties: To act as hostess in dining room by:

1. Directing residents to tables.

2. Assisting residents in getting positioned at tables.

3. Being cognizant of special needs and moods of residents so as to help create a pleasant atmosphere.

This assignment can be combined with other volunteer assignments in the nursing home that will not interfere.

Qualifications: Pleasant appearance and personality, with empathy for older people.
Maturity in judgment and ability to cope with difficult situations.
Sense of humor.
Social graces.

Training requirements: Basic orientation.

Supervision:

Date:

VOLUNTEER SERVICE ASSIGNMENT GUIDE

Title: Reality orientation instructor   **Using service:** Occupational therapy

Assignment needs: Six to eight for teaching two half-hour classes daily;
each would instruct only one class daily.

Frequency: Weekly.

Hours: 9:30 to 10 a.m.   10:15 to 10:45 a.m.   11 to 11:30 a.m.
(Actual service is only 45 minutes in morning.)

Duties: 1. Conduct a class of five residents in reality orientation.
2. Help to draw out withdrawn patients.
3. Maintain an atmosphere in which residents regain a favorable
self-image.
4. Bring reality objects (leaf, flower, nest) to share briefly with class.
5. Assist therapists in locating and transporting residents to classroom.
6. Become familiar with pertinent information concerning
residents in class.

Qualifications: Sensitivity to others' needs.
Attitude of active friendliness.
Empathy, as opposed to sympathy.
Ability to listen.
Reliability.
Enjoyment of working with older persons.
Ability to give honest praise.

Training requirements: Basic orientation, which includes observing in
classroom for two sessions.

Supervision:

Date:

figure 39h
volunteer service
assignment guide
social activity aide
(bingo)

VOLUNTEER SERVICE ASSIGNMENT GUIDE

Title: Social activity aide (Bingo)   **Using service:** Activities

Assignment needs: A group of about 25.

Frequency: Weekly, on Saturdays.

Hours: 2 to 4:30 p.m.

Duties: To assist staff in conducting Bingo games by:

1. Setting up for the activity in auditorium.
2. Assisting in transportation of residents to activity.
3. Calling games and assisting residents in playing.
4. Giving prizes.
5. Serving refreshments.
6. Cleaning up following activity.

Qualifications: Youth groups preferred; minimum age: nine years.
Should enjoy working with older persons.
Should be prompt and dependable.
Should be well mannered.
Should have ability to follow instructions.

Training requirements: Group briefing by nursing home staff.

Supervision:

Date:

**figure 39i
volunteer service
assignment guide
staff aide (youth)**

VOLUNTEER SERVICE ASSIGNMENT GUIDE

Title: Staff aide (youth)   **Using service:** Activities

Assignment needs: Two or three for Saturdays during entire year (mornings).
Two or three daily during summer (afternoons).

Frequency: Weekly.

Hours: Saturdays: 9 a.m. to 12 noon (all year).
Weekdays: 1 p.m.

Duties: To assist staff:

1. In hobby house on Saturday mornings with arts and crafts.

2. In games or any needed activity during afternoons of summer months.

Qualifications: Must be at least 12 years old.
Must be dependable.
Must be neat.
Must be cooperative and able to deal with older persons.
Must have good attitude about assignment.

Training requirements: Basic orientation.

Supervision:

Date:

**figure 39j
volunteer service
assignment guide
staff aide
(admitting office)**

VOLUNTEER SERVICE ASSIGNMENT GUIDE

Title: Staff aide   **Using service:** Admitting office

Assignment needs: Seven, one for each day of the week.

Frequency: Weekly.

Hours: 9 a.m. to 3 p.m.

Duties: To assist in the admitting office by:
    1. Filling in social history forms of residents.
    2. Conducting tours.

Qualifications: Pleasing personality and appearance, with patience and
    empathy for older persons.
    Ability to evaluate pertinent information.
    Ability to type helpful, but not mandatory.
    Ability, with training, to speak intelligently about program and
    facilities of the nursing home, while conducting tours.

Training requirements: Basic orientation.
    Special training for conducting tours.

Supervision:

Date:

**figure 39k
volunteer service
assignment guide
staff aide
(physical therapy)**

VOLUNTEER SERVICE ASSIGNMENT GUIDE

Title: Staff aide   **Using service:** Physical therapy

Assignment needs: Two: one for Monday, one for Friday.

Frequency: Weekly.

Hours: 9 a.m. to 3:30 p.m.

Duties: To help in the physical therapy department when needed by:
1. Walking patients (when extra person is needed).
2. Preparing hot packs.
3. Running errands, primarily within department.
4. Making coffee and helping to keep area neat.

Qualifications: Must be at least 5'2" in height.
Must be able to follow instructions.
Must have compassion.
Must be flexible.
Must be agile.

Training requirements: Basic orientation.

Supervision:

Date:

figure 39l
volunteer service
assignment guide
transportation aide
(errands, shopping)

VOLUNTEER SERVICE ASSIGNMENT GUIDE

Title: Transportation aide   **Using service:** Activities
(errands, shopping)

Assignment needs: Six: one regular and five on call.

Frequency: Weekly.

Hours: Variable (daytime). Thursdays and Fridays for movie pickup;
every third Thursday for popcorn pickup; weekdays, as needed.

Duties: Pick up movie film.
Pick up popcorn.
Take residents to doctor's appointments.
Take residents shopping.
Shop for residents unable to leave nursing home.

Qualifications: Must have car and driver's license.
Must be patient and willing to help.

Training requirements: Basic orientation.

Supervision:

Date:

figure 39m
volunteer service
assignment guide
transportation aide
(group trips)

VOLUNTEER SERVICE ASSIGNMENT GUIDE

Title: Transportation aide (group trips) **Using service:** Activities

Assignment needs: Six: two used normally for a trip, four on call.

Frequency: Flexible.

Hours: Flexible. Days also flexible.

Duties: To assist staff with special off-station events and trips scheduled
for residents.
To assist in driving, if necessary.
To assist in getting residents in and out of van.
To supervise and aid residents in the activity at the destination.

Qualifications: Must have car and driver's license.
Must be physically able to assist residents in and out of van.
Must have cheerful disposition.
Must be able to remain calm under stress.

Training requirements: Basic orientation.

Supervision:

Date:

**figure 39n
volunteer service
assignment guide
art instructor**

VOLUNTEER SERVICE ASSIGNMENT GUIDE

Title: Art instructor   **Using service:** Activities

Assignment needs: One.

Frequency: Weekly.

Hours: To be determined.

Duties: To stimulate interest among residents in participating in art classes.
To instruct residents in various types of art expression.
To give classes in art appreciation.

Qualifications: Should be trained and experienced instructor in several facets
of art, with a knowledge of all.
Should be pleasant and stimulating.
Should have empathy for older persons—their interests,
capabilities, and tolerances.

Training requirements: Basic orientation.

Supervision:

Date:

**figure 39o
volunteer service
assignment guide
carpenter**

VOLUNTEER SERVICE ASSIGNMENT GUIDE

Title: Carpenter   **Using service:** Activities

Assignment needs: One, one day each week.

Frequency: Weekly.

Hours: To be determined.

Duties: To assist the activity staff by:
  1. Building equipment for use in arts and crafts shop.
  2. Building for other needs throughout the nursing home.

Qualifications: Should have woodworking shop of his own in which he can prepare the assignments of the activity staff.

Training requirements: Basic orientation.

Supervision:

Date:

figure 39p
volunteer service
assignment guide
choir leader

VOLUNTEER SERVICE ASSIGNMENT GUIDE

Title: Choir leader   **Using service:** Activities

Assignment needs: One.

Frequency: Weekly.

Hours: To be determined.

Duties: To develop a choir among the residents for performance at church services of the nursing home.

Qualifications: Should be an experienced choir director, with ability to read music.
Should be capable of placing emphasis on involvement of individuals rather than on quality of performance.
Should have empathy for older persons—their interests, abilities, and tolerances.

Training requirements: Basic orientation.

Supervision:

Date:

**figure 39q
volunteer service
assignment guide
clerical aide
(physical therapy)**

VOLUNTEER SERVICE ASSIGNMENT GUIDE

Title: Clerical aide   **Using service:** Physical therapy

Assignment needs: Five, one for each weekday.

Frequency: Weekly.

Hours: Three to six hours each day (9 a.m. to 3:30 p.m.)

Duties: To assist in office of the physical therapist by:
1. Logging in or listing patients' treatment schedules for the week.
2. Counting patients and treatments.
3. Filling out forms.

Qualifications: Accuracy in working with figures.
Typing helpful, but not mandatory.
Calm manner; ability to cope with working in a small area
when there seems to be confusion.

Training requirements: Basic orientation.

Supervision:

Date:

VOLUNTEER SERVICE ASSIGNMENT GUIDE

Title: Gardening aide   **Using service:** Activities

Assignment needs: One or two.

Frequency: Weekly.

Hours: To be determined.

Duties: To assist in:
1. Planting and caring for the gardening projects, both indoor and outdoor, for the nursing home.
2. Distributing and caring for flowers of residents.
3. Doing flower arrangements.
4. Involving residents in gardening activities when they are interested and have potential for such work.
5. Helping in planning new garden projects and shows.

Qualifications: Should enjoy and have knowledge of gardening, both indoor and outdoor.
Should be stimulating and friendly.
Should have empathy for older persons—their interests, capabilities, and tolerances.

Training requirements: Basic orientation.

Supervision:

Date:

**figure 39s
volunteer service
assignment guide
genealogy instructor**

VOLUNTEER SERVICE ASSIGNMENT GUIDE

Title: Genealogy instructor   **Using service:** Activities

Assignment needs: One.

Frequency: Weekly.

Hours: To be determined.

Duties: To interest residents in genealogy and to assist them in
developing this hobby.
To write letters for residents who are not capable of writing their own
in this project.

Qualifications: Should be experienced in the art of genealogy.
Should be stimulating and friendly.
Should have empathy for older persons—their interests,
capabilities, and tolerances.

Training requirements: Basic orientation.

Supervision:

Date:

**figure 39t
volunteer service
assignment guide
lapidary aide**

VOLUNTEER SERVICE ASSIGNMENT GUIDE

Title: Lapidary aide　　　　　　　　　**Using service:** Activities

Assignment needs: One.

Frequency: Weekly.

Hours: To be determined.

Duties: To assist residents in learning skills of lapidary as a hobby.

Qualifications: Must be experienced in the skill of cutting and polishing
precious and semiprecious stones.
Should be friendly and stimulating.
Should have empathy for older persons—their interests,
capabilities, and tolerances.

Training requirements: Basic orientation.

Supervision:

Date:

figure 39u
volunteer service
assignment guide
librarian

VOLUNTEER SERVICE ASSIGNMENT GUIDE

Title: Librarian   **Using service:** Activities

Assignment needs: Four: two for Mondays, two for Wednesdays.

Frequency: Weekly.

Hours: 9 a.m. to 11 a.m.
1 p.m. to 3 p.m.

Duties: Checking books in and out.
Taking book cart to rooms.
Nurturing an interest in books among the residents.
Being cognizant of special interests in various types of books.

Qualifications: Knowledge of and interest in literature and various types of
reading materials and tools.
Interest in working with residents.
Ability to be neat and orderly.

Training requirements: Basic orientation.

Supervision:

Date:

figure 39v
volunteer service
assignment guide
music accompanist

VOLUNTEER SERVICE ASSIGNMENT GUIDE

Title: Music accompanist　　　　　　**Using service:** Activities

Assignment needs: One.

Frequency: Weekly.

Hours: Varied, and to be determined.

Duties: To accompany community sings and choral groups.

Qualifications: Must be an experienced piano and/or autoharp accompanist, with ability to accompany community sings and choral groups.
Must be able to read music and preferably to transpose to different keys.

Training requirements: Basic orientation.

Supervision:

Date:

**figure 30w
volunteer service
assignment guide
photography aide**

VOLUNTEER SERVICE ASSIGNMENT GUIDE

Title: Photography aide   **Using service:** Activities

Assignment needs: One.

Frequency: Weekly.

Hours: To be determined.

Duties: 1. To take pictures of residents or of activities of the nursing home.
2. To develop pictures.
3. To interest residents in participating in photography as a hobby; to give them instructions and assignments when they have the interest and potential.

Qualifications: Experience in photography and darkroom developing.

Training requirements: Basic orientation.

Supervision:

Date:

**figure 39x
volunteer service
assignment guide
projectionist**

VOLUNTEER SERVICE ASSIGNMENT GUIDE

Title: Projectionist   **Using service:** Activities

Assignment needs: One, for Thursday evening.

Frequency: Weekly.

Hours: 6 p.m. to 9 p.m.

Duties: To show 16-mm movies to residents on Thursday evenings.

Qualifications: Preferably an experienced projectionist with ability to
splice film and make minor projector adjustments.
Will consider training an inexperienced person with the
potential for learning this skill.

Training requirements: Basic orientation.

Supervision:

Date:

**figure 39y
volunteer service
assignment guide
sewing aide**

VOLUNTEER SERVICE ASSIGNMENT GUIDE

Title: Sewing aide   **Using service:** Activities

Assignment needs: One, for any established day of choice.

Frequency: Weekly.

Hours: Any four hours of established choice.

Duties: To assist in mending housekeeping items and residents' clothing.
To assist in sewing projects for the hobby house.

Qualifications: Should have sewing ability and experience.

Training requirements: Basic orientation.

Supervision:

Date:

**figure 40
example of
request for
volunteer service**

REQUEST FOR VOLUNTEER SERVICE

Date _____   Department _____

Please state hours and number of volunteers needed
in appropriate box.

Day of Week	Morning	Afternoon	Evening
Sunday			
Monday			
Tuesday			
Wednesday			
Thursday			
Friday			
Saturday			

Comments:

Supervisor's signature:

_____

**figure 41
example of
30-second spot
for radio**

We care—it's as simple as that!

If you are serious about wanting to use your time in an important and worthwhile way, we invite you to join Swope Ridge Health Care Center's "We Care Team."

To be on this team requires just one important personal quality—caring about older persons.

If you care, Swope Ridge Health Care Center needs you. Call Mrs. Joann Zind at 333-2700 and ask how you can help. Show that you care.

**figure 42
example of
one-minute spot
for radio**

It's not too late to do something. Have you ever sat down for just a moment and wondered where the time goes? It seems a shame that we often don't get a chance to do the really worthwhile things we want and could do. Maybe we have an answer for you.

Would you give a few hours a week that may change your life, a few hours that would help someone else live a little better, a little happier? Swope Ridge Health Care Center needs you to become a charter member of our auxiliary. You would be part of a team that helps hundreds of older persons adjust to their daily life. The Swope Ridge Auxiliary offers you the good feeling that comes from giving of yourself and your time to help others and to serve your community. It offers you a chance to learn and to be an important part of a new concept in health care. Senator Eagleton commented recently that Swope Ridge serves the elderly not only with brick and mortar but also with concerned people dedicated to service.

Why not call Mrs. Joann Zind at Swope Ridge today for more information? The number is 333-2700. Or stop in and visit us at 59th and Swope Parkway. It just might make your day a lot brighter.

**figure 43
example of
volunteer
application form**

VOLUNTEER APPLICATION FORM

PLEASE PRINT

Date: _____

Name: _____
           Last   First   Middle   Name of Spouse

Address: _____ _____
         Number   Street   City   State   Zip   Phone

Age range: (If under 25, give exact age) _____ 25-35_____ 35-50 _____ Over 50 _____
Marital status: Single_____ Married_____ Divorced_____ Widowed_____
Children: How many_____ Ages_____

Present occupation: Title_____

                         Company_____

Previous work experience: _____

_____

Education: _____
            Indicate last grade completed   Year   Degrees
Vocational or special training: _____
Community and club affiliations: _____
Previous volunteer experience: _____
Reason for volunteering: _____

Condition of health: Excellent_____ Good_____ Fair_____
                     Height_____ Weight_____
Date of last physical exam: _____ Date of last chest x-ray: _____
Whom to call if ill: _____ _____
                          Name   Phone

References: 1. _____
                    Name   Address
         2. _____
                    Name   Address

Special skills: _____

Hobbies and interests: _____

Have car? Yes_____ No_____ Source of transportation: _____
Days and times available: _____

**figure 44
example of
volunteer
interview form**

VOLUNTEER INTERVIEW FORM
(To be completed by interviewer)

Available Time

	(Write actual time period.)			If not each week, designate 1st, 2nd . . . preference.
	Morning	Afternoon	Evening	
Sunday				
Monday				
Tuesday				
Wednesday				
Thursday				
Friday				
Saturday				
On call				

Initial interview by: _____ Date: _____

Using service interview by: _____ Date: _____

Original assignment: _____ Starting date: _____

Assignment changes: _____ Date: _____

_____ _____

_____ _____

_____ _____

_____ _____

_____ _____

_____ _____

**figure 45
example of
volunteer
sign-in record**

VOLUNTEER SIGN-IN RECORD

Month_____ **Year**_____

Name	Organization	Assignment	Date	Time in	Time out	Total

Page total_____ Previous total_____ Grand total for month_____

figure 46
example of
volunteer
vacation schedule

VOLUNTEER VACATION SCHEDULE

Name	Assignment	Vacation Period

The volunteer vacation schedule should be reported to the using service.

chapter 6
Life Activities

Life Activity Areas

This chapter focuses primarily on four life activity areas: continuing education, employment, recreation, and religion. After a brief discussion of these four areas, the rest of the chapter is devoted to the actual activities related to these areas. It should be noted that the specific activities described are not allocated to one or another of the four life activity areas, because in a truly coordinated program almost every activity serves a variety of needs and purposes.

Continuing Education

For many younger persons, the purpose of learning is academic or occupational advancement. Nursing home residents, however, participate purely for the fun, enjoyment, and satisfaction of learning. Therefore, many residents are, or can be, motivated to participate in educational activities, both formal and informal.

Opportunities that can be provided include classes, lectures, demonstrations, debates, exhibits, discussion groups, correspondence courses, audio-visual presentations, and activities directed to current events and public affairs. Such programs can help to improve skills, knowledge, attitudes, understanding, and appreciation. In addition, they can provide outlets for self-awareness and self-acceptance.

Employment

Older persons seem to derive considerable benefit from working for pay, even when the amount is small. This seems especially true of persons in the lower socioeconomic range. Results of a study by Carp indicate that "individuals who worked for pay were happier, had higher self-esteem, better relations with other people, and tended to complain less of having too much free time than did either the volunteers or those who were not in any employment."[1]

Employment opportunities for nursing home residents are limited. One possibility, however, is to establish a sheltered workshop for the residents. A sheltered workshop is a place of employment where the workers are protected from the high productivity pressures usually found in industry. Workers are paid commensurate with their levels of ability and production. Another possibility is to offer a stipend to residents working in the home, such as in the gift shop or on the switchboard. Residents with special talents may be motivated by cash awards to enter contests (writing, photography), do mending, or sell paintings. The activity director may be able to think of other activities for which residents might receive financial remuneration. However, the activity director should be sure to check with the administrator on questions concerning wage-hour laws.

Recreation

Recreation is an attitude, a way of life. It includes games and sports, music and drama, arts and crafts, reading and writing, and many other activities. Its value is deeper than just busywork or freedom from boredom. Recreation, like education and religion, provides opportunities for mental, physical, emotional, social, spiritual, and intellectual growth. It offers an opportunity for dignity and self-awareness. In other words, recreation allows a person to lead a fuller, more satisfying life.

Through the medium of activities and relationships, recreation has much to offer the aged and the chronically ill. Leisure hours not put to wise use produce a meaningless existence, but these hours put to good use permit each person to remain meaningful and purposeful to himself and to others.

Religion

Religious opportunities must be considered an integral part of the total care program. Belief in God and faith in His omnipotence give residents the spiritual strength with which to live the remaining part of their lives. A personal approach to religion recognizes individual rights and allows the interpretation and application to be determined by each individual. It further recognizes the individual's need to be needed, useful, serving, and loving, thus providing a sense of dignity and value. Religion is tied closely to education and recreation during all phases of life. It encourages growth and self-development regardless of age.

Structured church and religious activities are discussed later in this chapter; but it is important to remember that religion is not a separate activity, but relates to *all* of the activities and interactions of life.

Types of Programs

Because of the considerable diversity in the size, type, and location of activity programs, activities can be planned for one person, for small groups, and for large groups. Activities should include opportunities for both active and passive participation.

Activities can be held at the bedside, in a room, or in a ward. They can even take place in the community. Some can be indoors, others outdoors. Some are specifically recreational, educational, or religious; others are difficult to differentiate. Some are designed to be therapeutic; others are not.

An activity program can incorporate arts and crafts; audiovisual presentations; cooking and baking; current events and citizenship themes; dance; discussion groups, debates, and symposiums; drama; educational classes; entertainment; exercise; exhibits; games; hobbies; lectures and demonstrations; literature; music; nature and outdoor activities; outings and trips; parties; service projects; special events; sports; visitation programs; and worship services and religious observances. The multiplicity of opportunities should not be frightening, but rather should demonstrate the variety and scope available to meet the needs and interests of the residents.

If the program is to truly meet the residents' needs and interests, it is imperative that the residents be involved as much as possible in developing and planning the activities. Social histories, questionnaires, and other interest finders are helpful in planning. More direct involvement can be achieved by organizing resident committees to represent residents' views, either specifically for the activity program or possibly also for other areas, such as the food committee and the building and grounds committee. Such committees are especially impor-

---

[1]Carp, F. M. Differences among older workers, volunteers, and persons who are neither. *Journal of Gerontology.* 23: 497, Oct. 1968.

tant if the size of the nursing home warrants an increase in the number of involved residents.

The remainder of this chapter is devoted to discussion of the various types of activities. For convenience, the activities are listed alphabetically.

Arts and Crafts

Arts and crafts activities should consist of opportunities for the skilled and instruction for the interested but unskilled. Although some residents may be capable only of coloring, finger painting, or spatter painting, others may be familiar with oils or watercolors, or even tole painting or china painting. There may be residents who have created cartoons, caricatures, or sketches, or maybe even sculptures, etchings, or woodblocks.

Classes for beginners or for the advanced may stimulate a new or renewed interest. Trips to art exhibitions or to an art museum may nurture an interest in art. Art appreciation classes on the general field or a specific study stimulate a greater appreciation and understanding of art. In addition, films, slides, lectures, and discussions are enjoyable as well as informative.

One of the most common activities found in nursing homes is a program of crafts. Crafts dealing in the manual arts provide many desirable outlets for older persons. Needs for self-expression, creativity, intellectual stimulation, and physical movement can be fulfilled through an interesting and diversified crafts program. Such a program can also serve as a substitute for a former occupation.

Many persons continue to generalize their belief that older persons prefer short-term projects that are not too difficult. Caution should be exercised in accepting such a belief. Each resident must be considered individually. At Swope Ridge it has been found that *projects requiring more time and effort often can be of more interest and value to the long-term resident who has already completed a number of short remedial projects.*

Craft projects can be simple or complex, inexpensive or costly. How to finance the projects is a question that each nursing home must answer for itself. The following different methods of charging can be considered:

- The cost of supplies is absorbed in the general rate.
- The cost of supplies used by residents is charged to them.

- The cost of supplies used by residents is charged to them. Then at the completion of their project they have the privilege of (1) keeping the article or (2) placing the article for sale. If the item is made available for sale, the resident receives the money after it is sold. Each item sold covers the cost of materials plus a charge for the labor and skill that went into making the item. Therefore, as an example, if the materials used cost 50 cents, the resident is billed for 50 cents, and a sales tag for $1 is placed on the item. When and if the item is sold, the resident receives the $1 from the sale, which amounts to a profit of 50 cents.
- The cost of supplies is assumed by the institution. Completed items then belong to the institution and can be sold regularly or at an annual bazaar, with the money directed back into the program.
- A resident makes two of the same item. One becomes his own; the other becomes the property of the institution and is sold for twice the amount of the cost of materials. This pays for the cost of supplies in both items.

Many different materials can be used in creating craft products (figure 47, page 124). Various items can even be developed from scraps and donated materials. When scraps are used, it is desirable to supplement the program with materials of better quality. More opportunities are then available to stimulate a variety of personal interests.

Specific arts and crafts projects that can be undertaken include copper tooling (figure 48, page 128), decoupage (figure 49, page 129), gravel mosaic pictures (figure 50, page 130), and leather lacing (figure 51, page 131). Products made from scrap materials include recipe or card holders (figure 52, page 132), greeting cards (figure 53, page 133), wastebaskets (figure 54, page 134), cannisters (figure 55, page 134), pinecone flowers (figure 56, page 135), and flower plaques (figure 57, page 135).

To organize an arts and crafts program, the activity director (or other leader) should take the following preparatory steps:

1. Be sure that the area to be used for the program is well lighted and ventilated.
2. Consider the capabilities of the residents.
3. Find out what arts or crafts each resident now enjoys or enjoyed in the past.

4. Decide, in cooperation with the residents, what projects can be done. Select about three or four different projects to start with.

5. Survey the community to find additional information on arts and crafts programs, and contact sources, including volunteers, who will donate needed materials, supplies, tools, equipment, and so forth.

6. Purchase materials, supplies, tools, and equipment that are not available free of charge.

7. Make, or somehow get a sample of, the projects, in order to show the residents how the completed projects look.

8. Become familiar with the steps necessary to complete each project.

9. Arrange for any aids that specific residents may require in order to work on the project.

10. Find out about special projects that can be accomplished by the disabled.

The following suggestions should be helpful to the activity director in carrying out a specific arts or crafts activity. The procedure can be followed with a small group of residents who are working on the same project or on different projects. Residents in their rooms can also be involved in working on a project at bedside. If they can, they should be encouraged to come out of their rooms to do their work.

1. Show a finished sample to residents who are interested or who are being encouraged to start the project.

2. Demonstrate the first step.

3. Position the residents properly.

4. Ask them to repeat the first step, and offer any suggestions or help that will be useful to them. Make sure they understand and are capable of doing as instructed.

5. Check periodically to see that each person is working successfully on the project; help as needed. The director should be available regularly until he is satisfied that the resident can proceed alone.

6. Follow suggestions 2, 3, and 4 on all subsequent steps until the project is completed. Only help; never do the project for the residents.

7. When a project is being put away for the day, be sure it is labeled with the resident's name or placed in a box with the resident's name clearly marked.

Audiovisual Presentations

Films, slides, records, and tape recordings are media for entertainment and information. Residents enjoy motion pictures, especially feature films. Feature films are generally available only through commercial rental companies. The prices vary for these 16-mm films, but normally the minimum rental cost is between $15 and $25 each. If funds are available, the activity staff may wish to investigate the cost of renting one film each month. Often, 16-mm short films can be borrowed from the public library or a sponsored film section of a film rental firm. Travel, health, music, history, religion, science, and art are but a few of the hundreds of subjects that can be presented through the use of these films.

Slide shows and multimedia presentations are another means of depicting places, people, or things. People who take slides will happily consent to give a showing with narration. In addition to individuals, sometimes groups such as "Armchair Travelers" can provide the source for such programs. Time for discussion should be allotted. Often, previously prepared questions will stimulate the discussion.

Records and tape recordings of events, as well as music, can be included as part of a program or can be a full program. Records can be taken out on loan from many libraries. Individuals will sometimes be happy to loan their records if the nursing home does not have a record library of its own.

It should be remembered that tape recorders can be used not only to provide interesting sound background for programs but also by individual residents, who often delight in recording and hearing their own voices.

The equipment required for a film program includes a 16-mm motion picture projector, a motion picture screen, a take-up reel, and spare projector parts. The activity director (or other leader) should take the following steps to organize a film program:[2]

1. Review the list of films available, and make a selection.

---

[2]Steps 4 through 13 are suggestions from Modern Talking Picture Service, 1836 Elmhurst Rd., Elk Grove Village, IL 60007.

2. A month or two weeks in advance, call or write to reserve the films.

3. Consider the best location for the program. If films are shown in the daytime, windows should have shades or blinds in order to darken the area.

4. Make sure that the source of electric power for the projector is supplied from a circuit that is separate from the one feeding the house lights. Otherwise, there is the possibility of blowing a fuse.

5. Place the projector so that the picture from the projector's lens fills the movie screen. Try to locate it in a position where it will not be in the way as the audience arrives and leaves the meeting room.

6. Run a final check on the projector itself while previewing the film. Clean the projection lens and film gate if specks of dust are found on the screen. The picture should be in focus and the film ready to run before the meeting starts.

7. If they are not provided with the projector, secure a spare projection lamp and exciter bulb from the audiovisual dealer as spares for emergencies. Make certain they can be installed with minimum delay for the audience. Spare springs should also be available.

8. Make sure that the take-up reel is as large as or larger than the one holding the film. Otherwise, film will spill out of the machine onto the floor, and needless work in rewinding it by hand will be necessary.

9. Place the loudspeaker in a position that enables everyone in the meeting room to hear it.

10. Test the sound level for the projector. Experiment to find the level that is most pleasing for the size of the room.

11. Shield the movie screen from any possible drafts or air currents that might cause a wavy picture.

12. Tape the projector cord to the floor with masking tape to avoid the possibility of falls.

13. Coordinate signals between the projectionist and others designated to help.

The following suggestions apply to a specific film showing:

1. Begin the film near the time announced.

2. If more than one reel of film is used, do not rewind the first reel as it is completed. Rather, take the full reel off, place the empty reel in its take-up position, and put on the second reel. The same procedure should be followed for any additional reels.

3. If desirable, serve popcorn or other refreshments during the show. Intermission, while the reel is being changed, is a good time to serve.

Cooking and Baking

Many female residents have spent a great part of their lives keeping house, cooking, and caring for themselves and others. Opportunities to continue these homemaking activities should be available to substitute for these past responsibilities. Preparing food, either individually or as a group project, eating it, and cleaning up can be a very enjoyable experience.

Examples of relatively simple activities for groups wishing to prepare foods include making popcorn, salads, candy, cookies, pizza, jelly, and corn bread. Equipment and supply limitations should be explained to residents, who then should be allowed to decide what they would like to make.

Lectures and demonstrations on subjects such as home economics, interior decorating, cake decorating, and so forth can supplement the do-it-yourself activities. A representative of the local university extension center, a home economics teacher, or a housewife can be invited to give a program. A resident may request or be invited to do the same.

Films are available on home living, cooking, foods and nutrition, grooming, fitness, health, and fashions.

To organize a cooking project, the activity director (or other leader) should:

1. Consider the capabilities of the residents and how much time will be reserved for the activity.

2. Decide what will be cooked or baked.

3. Get the recipe that will be used. Consider the length of time needed for the project, and choose a recipe simple enough to complete. Two or more sessions might be planned: for example, one for mixing dough, one for baking.

4. Arrange for needed supplies and equipment.

5. Order the ingredients.

6. Consider the seating arrangement. Provide for ample table space for all to participate.

7. Do any necessary preparation suggested in the recipe that is not to be done by residents.

8. Make a list of persons on special diets—for example, diabetics—who need to watch their intake of certain foods.

9. Print the recipe on the blackboard or the bulletin board so it is visible to residents.

To conduct a specific cooking activity, the leader should:

1. See that all participating residents have washed their hands thoroughly.

2. Help the residents put on aprons.

3. Make sure each resident has a function: stirring, mixing, cutting, icing, buttering, pouring, shaking, and so forth. For some cooking programs, it may be helpful to divide the group into several sections, with each section having a particular task to complete. For other projects, an individual may want to work alone.

4. When the food item is ready for cooking, baking, or whatever, make sure that recipe instructions are followed.

5. Begin the second batch, or if the proper amount has been prepared, use the waiting time for music, readings, or just visiting.

6. When the project is completed, see to it that it is shared with all those who assisted or were present at the program.

7. Allow residents to help clean up, wash dishes if possible, sweep the floor, and carry out other tasks that need to be done.

8. End the program.

Instead of completing the item and eating it themselves, the residents may want to use it for refreshments at a party or other event or at dinner. As another alternative, the residents may want to contribute prepared items to a community organization, for a bake sale, for example.

Current Events and Citizenship

Advanced communications systems keep the public informed of what is happening in the community, state, nation, and planet. Like other members of the community, nursing home residents, as long as they are mentally and emotionally able, have an obligation to be aware of current events.

Radio, television, and newspapers are the chief sources of news. Although the first two generally pose no problem, difficulties with vision often hinder older persons in reading the news. They can use magnifying glasses or other aids that are available. Large-print reading material is one possibility; the *New York Times* and *Reader's Digest* are available in enlarged type.

News program

A daily news program presented in the home, with commentary by a staff member or a volunteer, is a possible offering. Such a program need be only about 30 minutes; during this time several paragraphs of the top stories can be read. In addition to the news, weather, and sports, special activities planned for that day in the home can be announced.

In the case of morning papers, a reading in the dining area when residents are eating breakfast is desirable. If this is impractical, readings can be given at other times when a large group of residents is together. If only an evening paper is available, other satisfactory times should be considered. If an intercom system is available, its use would be advantageous. The use of a microphone would enable those in their rooms or other areas to hear and would also be an aid for any residents with hearing difficulties.

To conduct a news program, the activity director (or other leader) should:

1. Skim over the newspaper. Mark the first three, four, or five paragraphs of interesting articles (approximately 10 news items in all). Mark the weather forecast and the first couple of paragraphs from the financial section. Mark the first paragraph of the top two or three sports items. If the paper carries a syndicated column by Ann Landers, for example, mark this section. Also, if there is a section on events of the past, such as 5, 10, 25, or 40 years ago, prepare to read it.

2. Tear out the pages to be used, and put them in the order they will be read.

3. If possible, hook up a public address system so that, in addition to the immediate group, residents in their rooms can hear.

4. At the beginning of the program, give the day, date, year, and time.

5. Read the selected news reports, the weather report, the financial report, and the sports report. If desired, have a one-minute coffee break at this point.

6. Read other special columns planned. If a column such as Ann Landers is used, ask several residents their opinions prior to reading the columnist's reply.
7. Announce activities that will be available in the nursing home that day.
8. On Sunday, add one of the comic strips to the program. Read and describe the cartoon action.

Voting

Residents continue to have responsibility as citizens and must be encouraged to vote, as long as they are mentally and emotionally capable. Information gained from a good current events program can assist them in voting wisely.

Qualifications for voting vary in different states, counties, and precincts. The qualifications can be checked by calling the Board of Election Commissioners in the area. If it is not possible for residents to go out and vote, absentee ballot applications can be obtained from the election board. The election board should be contacted several weeks in advance of the election in order to make sure that the prescribed procedure is followed.

It is possible for residents to work in campaigns if they are so inclined and capable. Those interested could contact their local party headquarters to find out what they could do. By keeping up with issues in all areas of government, they can also let their representatives know their opinions.

Residents' council

Residents have duties, rights, and privileges regarding not only their government but also the nursing home itself. A form of democratic government can be established with help from the administration. The leaders of this government make up what is normally called a residents' council.

The purpose of the council is to provide the opportunity for residents to voice their opinions, comments, suggestions, criticisms, and compliments concerning the environment in which they live. It encourages them to participate in the planning, organizing, and directing, whenever possible, in order to maintain a degree of control over their daily activities. The residents' council consists of a group of residents who have been appointed, or preferably elected, chairmen of various committees organized within the nursing home.

Ideally the residents' council should have its own set of bylaws (figure 58, page 136).

The council, which should meet at least monthly, should be open to all residents who wish to attend. It is advisable for the executive director or administrator to meet with this body of representatives. The residents' council is designed to help the administrator keep a finger on the pulse of residents' opinion; to be aware of the committees' activities; and, most of all, to help him see things from the residents' point of view.

The number of committees on the council should be determined somewhat by the census of the nursing home and other factors. Possibly the council members will make up the only committee. In large institutions it is desirable to establish committees responsible for a specific phase of the environment, such as recreation, education, religion, hospitality, food, and building and grounds. Small institutions may prefer to combine some of these suggested committees. The important thing, however, is to provide an outlet for residents' views to be heard and their questions answered.

If committees are to be organized, responsibilities such as the following might be considered.

Recreation committee. Members work with the activity director in formulating and evaluating the program. They suggest new activities and assist in carrying out the activities. Members assume responsibility for greeting guests, writing thank-you letters, helping with program preparations, taking leadership roles in the programs, and tidying up the area.

Food committee. Members work with the dietitian in establishing the menus. Special and favorite dishes are discussed. The committee obtains the general reaction of other residents to the food and service, investigates complaints, and discusses problems with the dietitian. The dietitian is obligated to confer with the committee as to the reason she cannot serve certain dishes or take specific actions.

Religion committee. Members remind and encourage residents to attend religious services. Members may be involved in the services by leading hymns or saying prayers. They are active in special religious observances, Bible study or Sunday School groups, and other related activities.

Education committee. Members suggest topics for classes, lectures, demonstrations, workshops, exhibits, film and slide discussion groups, and other such activities. They accept responsibilities in carrying out these programs, evaluate them, and offer suggestions to overcome problems.

Welcoming committee. Members call on new residents to welcome them and assure them that the home desires to treat each resident as an individual. Traveling with basket-in-arm, a committee member may present a new resident with a welcoming letter from the council chairman, a change-of-address kit from the post office, an information sheet from the weather bureau containing norms on area weather conditions, and stationery and postcards. It is also worth while to solicit sample toiletries from local companies to include in the welcome kit. This committee may also sponsor a monthly tea for new residents.

Building and grounds committee. Members help to maintain and improve the appearance of the building. At regular intervals they make an inspection tour to ensure that standards of cleanliness and sanitation are maintained in the home. The committee reports to and makes recommendations to the housekeeping supervisor or other designated persons.

Dance

Many older persons enjoy dancing. With encouragement, they can be stimulated to take part in simple ballroom dances or easy square dances. Instruction programs can be planned for those persons who remain physically capable of participating. Wheelchair square dancing is possible with the assistance of volunteers. The spectators as well as the participants enjoy such programs. Live dance music is always preferred, but records can be used. Records are especially good for classes.

Leadership is the key to successful instruction. For square dancing, a caller, not necessarily a professional, is necessary, because calls from records are too fast. A staff member or volunteer just beginning should practice in advance before calling a square dance.

Individuals or groups can be invited to perform dance exhibitions in the nursing home. Square dance clubs can be invited to bring a set or two for demonstrations. Dance instructors can demonstrate ballroom dances. Dance studios generally seek opportunities for their students to gain experience performing before groups. The activity director should attempt to offer the highest quality possible.

Other dance forms, such as folk, tap, ballet, acrobatic, and modern, can be incorporated into a program, or one type can be a full program in itself. Even drill teams can demonstrate their patterns and maneuvers, especially on patriotic holidays. The American Legion, Veterans of Foreign Wars, American War Mothers, and high schools are but a few examples of possible contacts.

Dance appreciation classes and films offer other possibilities. In metropolitan areas commercial enterprises may present touring dance troupes. An outing could possibly be arranged for such a cultural treat, either on a complimentary basis or with each person paying his own admission.

Ballroom dancing

A dance instruction program can be planned prior to having a dance band perform at the nursing home so that many residents will be able to participate. In addition, ballroom dances can be planned periodically for those who already dance and do not require preinstruction. Live music is far preferable to records. An attractive decor for the walls, ceiling, and tables does much to encourage participation in such events.

To prepare for a ballroom dancing program, the activity director (or other leader) should:

1. Consider residents' limitations; then determine what type of dancing they enjoy and what they are capable of doing.
2. Arrange to have a record player.
3. Find records appropriate to the dance selected.
4. Become thoroughly familiar with the steps and how the instruction will be presented.
5. Prepare to have helpers available, if possible.

To conduct a ballroom dancing program, the leader should follow this sequence:

1. Begin by announcing to the participating residents the step that has been planned.
2. Line the men up facing the women, but several feet apart.
3. Demonstrate the women's step without music. Then ask them to follow. Let the women continue practicing.
4. While the women continue, show the men their step. Follow the same pattern as sug-

gested for the women. Let them practice for a minute or so.

5. Put on the selected record, and let both groups continue practicing independently. Assist each person in time with the music.
6. After a brief period, stop the music and have the men and women face one another and then walk forward until they are standing in front of their partners.
7. Demonstrate the proper ballroom dance position.
8. See that all are in proper position.
9. Without music, have the couples practice the step they have just learned or reviewed. Help those having problems.
10. Turn on the music and have them dance.
11. If they are doing fairly well, ask them to change partners and continue.
12. If more than one step is to be taught, see that they have learned the first; then ask that they return to their lines and follow the same procedure as followed with the first step.

Wheelchair square dancing

The equipment needed for wheelchair square dancing includes a phonograph, square dance records (instrumental), and, if possible, a microphone.

In preparation for a wheelchair square dance, the activity director (or other leader) should take the following steps:

1. Have records available that are suitable to square dancing and that do not already have the calls on them. (Square dance calls on records are too fast and not adaptable to the needs of the residents.)
2. Pick appropriate dances.
3. Become familiar with the calls, and make adaptations to simplify the dances as necessary.
4. Arrange enough volunteers or staff members so that each performing resident in a wheelchair (eight in all) will have someone to push him.
5. Orient the helpers to the plans, and demonstrate the moves to them.
6. Have plenty of space for maneuvering.

To conduct a wheelchair square dancing program, the leader should follow this sequence:

1. Turn the music on as residents enter the area. If more women than men are involved, the women who are taking male parts could wear cowboy hats if the group prefers that a differentiation be made.
2. Seek eight residents who will volunteer to participate in the first dance. Staff members or volunteers can encourage them.
3. Verbally guide participants through the dance first, without music, so all will know what they are to do.
4. Encourage residents, both participating and watching, to clap along with the music.
5. Start the music, and begin the calls.
6. When the first dance is over, change residents if possible, guide the dancers verbally through the next step without music, turn on the music, and begin calling while residents and volunteers engage in the action.
7. Follow step 6 on all future square dance numbers as they are changed.
8. End the program at about the time planned.

A refreshment break could be held midway through the program. Refreshments such as cider and doughnuts go well if there are no special diet problems.

If this activity proves to be popular, it could be offered periodically, or a small club that would meet regularly could be organized.

Discussion Groups, Debates, and Symposiums

Discussion groups allow residents to share ideas, experiences, and knowledge. One advantage of this type of program is that it encourages participation by the residents. In the beginning residents may choose to meet only with other residents, but later outside guests might be invited to participate. Topics such as "Problems That Face Our Nation: Crime, Civil Rights, Poverty, War, and Population," or other issues closer to the residents, can be selected. For subjects like "The Generation Gap," young people could be invited to give their views and answer questions.

Controversial topics should be kept issue-centered rather than person-centered. It is often wise and valuable for the leader to do some preliminary investigation to keep the session moving. However, he should be cautious not to dominate the discussion but, rather, should make brief, personally uncommitted statements to stimulate others to talk about the topics.

Debates and symposiums on controversial subjects can be informational to residents. Representatives from schools, political organizations, and the residents can be used to present different points of view. Examples include such topics as: "Should there be a guaranteed annual income for all citizens?" and "Which candidate is best qualified to hold office?"

In preparation for a small group discussion, the activity director (or other leader) should:

1. Select the topic or topics to be discussed.
2. Research the topics if necessary, in order to be prepared with adequate information. Residents can be assigned books or articles to read.
3. Plan the seating arrangement. A circle, preferably around a table, is a good arrangement. A microphone may be helpful.

At the beginning of the discussion, the leader should welcome the residents and, if necessary, help them with seating and arranging wheelchairs. The leader should initiate the discussion by presenting an introduction to the topic. Then discussion by the residents should be encouraged as the leader eases out of the limelight.

If pauses occur, the leader should not always feel compelled to speak. The quiet period may cause some discomfort among the group, but someone will generally break the silence and return the group to discussing the subject. If the conversation goes astray to other subjects, the leader should be prepared to return the group to the original topic.

In dealing with controversial subjects, violent conflicts should not be allowed to evolve. On the other hand, if interest lags, communication should be stimulated. If interest resumes, discussion should continue until the scheduled time to stop. If not, the leader should summarize and conclude the program.

Drama

Drama not only includes the production of plays but also offers many other program possibilities. This general heading includes pantomimes, skits, choral readings, musical productions, pageants, and reviews. Mock trials, weddings, elections, and so forth can also be very entertaining. It is possible to incorporate several forms of dramatics into one program to maintain audience interest. Residents not only can take acting roles but also can work on lighting, sound, costumes, and props. These activities are of special value to the participating residents and of unusual interest to the resident audience because they know the players.

Outside groups, including professional units on tour, drama clubs, little theaters, schools, churches, or other organizations, are potential sources for programs. These groups can be invited to perform at the nursing home, or a request could be made for complimentary admission (or a reduced rate) to their theater performances. Permission to attend a dress rehearsal is often given, because the actors benefit from playing to an audience. Recordings of great plays may be available in the public library. Many films can also be considered for use.

To organize a drama group and present a production, the activity director (or other leader) should:

1. Consider the possibilities of organizing short plays, dramatic readings, pantomimes, and skits.
2. Stimulate, motivate, and encourage residents to participate in a planning meeting.
3. At the meeting present pertinent information and specific ideas. Discuss the different possibilities with the residents, and try to get a feeling of what they are most interested in doing.
4. Determine what the residents are capable of doing, and learn what they want to do within the framework of their capabilities.
5. Have tryouts; select or vote on who will take the various roles. If a resident is capable of directing, let him or her do so; otherwise, assign a staff member or a volunteer who is knowledgeable and enthusiastic.
6. Set the date for the performance.
7. Get the books, or whatever contains the material, to be used. Possibly a resident could even write an original play. Type the material, preferably in large type. Mimeograph the number of copies needed.
8. Give the material to the cast members so they can read it over and practice alone.
9. Organize supplementary committees as needed, such as lighting, sound, music, props, publicity, costumes, and makeup.
10. Prepare these groups or persons to assume their responsibilities.

11. Hold rehearsals in order for the cast to practice together.
12. Supervise and assist those committees preparing for the event.
13. Have a dress rehearsal for the cast; use all that has been prepared. Have a prompter in the wings to help those who forget some of their lines.
14. Make any last-minute preparations or changes.
15. Present the production to an audience of residents, families, and visitors.
16. Close the curtains or leave the stage area. Have the cast come back to recognize the applause. Introduce each member of the cast and all who helped with the production.

Educational Classes

Formal classes can be developed on numerous subjects, but meaningful topics will come only from knowing the interests of the residents. Possibilities include music, politics, understanding people, current events, etiquette, travel, art, comparative religions, and sewing. The classes should not be purely academic, but can be for the purpose of enjoyment, enrichment, and the satisfaction of learning.

Those capable of instructing such classes include hobbyists, instructors, and other interested individuals.

A sample outline of a formally organized and structured course in music appreciation is included for reference (figure 59, page 138). A different type of class structure would be required for a sewing class. With the sewing group an informally arranged environment would be more suitable. This would permit participants to receive individual attention and assistance in addition to group instruction. Residents can work on the same project or separate projects.

Hixson indicates that emphasis should be placed on creating a nonclassroom atmosphere, that the comfort of the students should be placed ahead of the subject matter, that homework should never be assigned, and that threatening terms should not be used.[3] He states that "Some of the factors that seem to exert great influence in this nonthreatening approach include the learning environment, the teacher method, orientation of the learning process,

psychological interactions, semantics, and motivation." These are points worth considering.

To organize several educational classes, the activity director (or other leader) should:
1. Determine from the residents what subjects would most interest them.
2. Contact a local junior college, college, university, or university extension division to investigate the possibility of utilizing students to teach classes. (Consider school teachers, current and retired; housewives with special training, experience, or skills; business people; and students, who would be particularly helpful if they could receive teaching credit such as they would receive in a seminar practicum class.)
3. Once the courses are decided upon and the instructors selected, schedule a meeting with the instructors.
4. Provide the instructors with an orientation to the nursing home, and acquaint them with the residents. This helps the instructors determine the level of instruction. During this period acquaint the instructors with special problems and difficulties that are sure to be encountered with the residents, the physical plant, and so forth. Remind them generally not to make the material too technical, but to attempt to relate the material to the residents and to encourage residents' participation. Offer other information that might be valuable, and answer questions the instructors may have. Decide whether the classes are to meet once a week or twice a week, at what times and where. Also decide on the length of time the classes will run.
5. Arrange for any supplies that will be needed.
6. Determine the best classroom arrangement.
7. Announce the coming class programs to residents.
8. Have each instructor prepare a class outline for the semester or other period. The outline can be altered as needed.

At the beginning of the first class session, the activity director should introduce the instructor. The instructor should then tell a little about himself and ask that each student give his name and share other pertinent information. This helps the instructor determine how to teach the class and at what level. Then the instructor should verbally

[3]Hixson, L. E. Non-threatening education for older adults. *Adult Leadership.* 18:84, Sept. 1969.

outline the plan for the course and present a general approach to the subject. The first session may be short; the second class session should be full length.

Homework should be optional, depending on the abilities of the residents. It is probably best not to have tests; they may be too threatening.

Certificates could be presented to those who complete the course. If so, the only criterion should be the number of classes attended.

Entertainment

Entertainment encompasses a variety of activities that cross the lines of other topics discussed in this chapter. It may involve athletic contests; any of the performing arts, such as music, dance, and drama; or more unusual forms. Residents with talent should be encouraged to perform for other residents and, when possible, for community organizations. When several residents are talented, a variety show can be produced utilizing residents only, or residents and staff.

Entertainment can involve a performance by one person or many. On some occasions, entertainment might make up an entire program. At other times, entertainment might be used as only part of a program to highlight a party or other social event.

Within the community there may be professional entertainers, or persons with avocations such as clowns, magicians, acrobats, impersonators, comedians, jugglers, or baton twirlers. There may be others who do card tricks, produce puppet or marionette shows, have dog acts, or perform Indian or hula dances. The activity director should check with schools, clubs, fraternal organizations, and military bases and inform them of the kinds of entertainment desired. Newspapers and other media are good sources of information on entertainers.

Most people enjoy many forms of entertainment as spectators. In planning entertainment, however, the activity director should not rely heavily on passive spectatorship and overlook resident participation.

To organize and conduct an entertainment program, the activity director (or other leader) should:

1. Develop a file of talented groups and individuals. Jot down on 3-inch by 5-inch cards the name of the person to contact and his telephone number and address. Indicate the specific type of skill or talent the person or group has, and note the reference, if any, for obtaining this information. Include any additional comments that will be helpful.

2. Determine whether the entertainment will be presented as a full program or as part of a program.

3. Consider the time and the date that the program will be offered. Be prepared with one or two alternative dates in case the preferred date is unacceptable to the contact.

4. Call the contact person approximately a month to two weeks in advance of the time the program is scheduled. After a simple introduction, briefly describe the planned program and its purpose, and then invite the individual or group to entertain, suggesting the date previously considered. If the person accepts the invitation, give additional information as to the time of the program, location of the facility, and the area in which the performance will be given. If the person needs equipment, such as a piano or a record player, indicate what is available. Thank the person, and indicate that he will receive a letter confirming the arrangements.

5. Approximately a week prior to the program, send the confirmation letter. Reaffirm the telephone arrangements, giving the who, what, when, where, and why.

6. Prepare the area for the event prior to the program.

7. Make the final announcement of the activity to the residents one-half to one hour prior to starting time, depending on how long it will take to get the residents to the area where the activity will be held.

8. Anticipate the arrival of the guest, and be prepared to personally greet him and go over any final arrangements. Take his hat, coat, and so forth. Assist with any equipment brought for the program.

9. With interest and enthusiasm, introduce the person or group who will perform to the resident audience.

10. After the introduction, take care of any tasks that must be performed, such as opening stage curtains, starting a phonograph, turning on a spotlight, and the like. If possible, sit in the audience with the residents. Dis-

play interest by being attentive to the performance, applauding, laughing, or whatever at appropriate times.

11. After the performance, thank the performer on behalf of the entire audience.

12. Thank the performer personally after he has finished or is about to leave. Offer to help carry out any equipment brought along for use in the program.

13. Offer other courtesies that may be appropriate both before and after the activity.

An example of an entertainment program along the lines of the "Tonight" show is included for reference (figure 60, page 141).

Exercise

Physical conditioning programs for selected residents should be scheduled regularly. If the physical therapy department does not sponsor such a program, the activity department could do so. The type of exercises planned should be geared to the physical tolerance and capabilities of the residents. Exercises can be developed for residents who can stand up. Different variations should be considered for those who must remain seated. Plans should be discussed with doctors, nurses, and physical therapists for their reactions and suggestions.

Exercise increases efficiency, endurance, balance, flexibility, coordination, and agility.[4] It permits older persons to function better in the normal activities of living as well as in other activities offered by nursing homes.

Taking regular or periodic walks when weather is good is valuable not only from the exercise standpoint but also for other physical and emotional reasons. Safety precautions must be taken; it may be necessary to have one staff member or volunteer for each resident. Restraining belts should be used on persons subject to falls. Helpers need to be familiar with any hazards in the walk area, such as curbs, cracked sidewalks, and so forth, to give notice to the residents who may fail to see them. Residents confined to wheelchairs can also be taken on walks. The procedure for obtaining medical approval is described under Outings and Trips, page 118. In a nursing home with a physical ther-

apy department, the activity staff may be able to receive assistance from that department.

To organize an exercise program, the activity director or other staff member should make a list of the desired exercises and become familiar with how to do each exercise.

A group exercise program developed for residents confined to wheelchairs is included for reference (figure 61, page 142). Because the exercises are rhythmic, they may be done to recorded music or live piano music.

Exhibits

Exhibits provide opportunities for enrichment. Exhibits of art, antiques, crafts, new products, and flowers are possible. They may be brought by individuals, clubs, organizations, industries, residents, their families, or employees.

A well-devised method of receiving items for exhibit and returning the items to owners is imperative. Arrangements for insurance and security provide protection to the institution and can ward off potential problems. Changeable displays, such as art works in a library or arts and crafts in a particular location, might be considered.

To organize an exhibit, the activity director (or other leader) should:

1. Announce the date and time of the exhibit a month in advance to individuals or groups whose items are to be exhibited, preferably residents, relatives, and friends. Also state the deadline for receiving items.

2. Make individual contacts and calls to ensure that at least a minimum number of items will be available for showing.

3. Prepare 3-inch by 5-inch cards that note the owner's name, telephone number, the date the item was received, who received it, any history or information about the item, and the date it will be picked up by the owner.

4. Consider the need for insurance and police protection for the exhibit.

5. Plan how the items will be exhibited. If necessary, make or rent risers.

6. Prepare signs stating "Please Do Not Handle" and, if necessary, signs saying "Entrance" and "Exit."

7. Make or buy a book for guests to use for registering.

[4]The President's Council on Physical Fitness and Sports and the Administration on Aging. *The Fitness Challenge ...in the Later Years* (AOA Publication No. 802). Washington, DC: Administration on Aging, May 1968.

8. Arrange for a resident hostess to handle the registration table and for other residents to greet visitors.

9. Order refreshments, and arrange for residents to serve them.

10. As items are received, complete the cards mentioned in step 3. In order that exhibit items are properly stored and protected, they should be received not more than 24 to 48 hours prior to program time.

11. Prior to the exhibit, type up index cards giving the owner's name, the history, and other information of interest. Place the cards next to the corresponding items.

12. Limit other activities during the period the exhibit is shown.

13. Arrange for a speaker or someone to explain the exhibit.

14. Attractively arrange the articles for exhibit.

15. Complete any last-minute details.

During the exhibit, the activity director should make sure that:

1. The resident assistants are at their proper locations.

2. The exhibit is opened at the scheduled time.

3. All who attend sign the guest register.

4. Any special plans that have been arranged, such as a guest speaker, are carried out.

5. Refreshments are served as planned.

6. The exhibit closes at the scheduled time.

Games

There are many types and kinds of games. Cards, chess, and checkers, and games like Monopoly® and Scrabble® are probably the most common. Quiet games, active games, mental games, and puzzles are available, some at minimal cost and others expensive, some played on a table and others on the floor. In addition, many residents enjoy parlor games, paper games, and quiz games.

For residents who prefer to play games by themselves or with one or more friends in their rooms or other locations, equipment should be readily accessible. Game programs for small or large groups can be held in the recreation area. If desired and feasible, prizes can be awarded to the winners.

The following additional suggestions might be helpful in organizing games:

1. More than one game can be planned for the period if games can be completed in a short

time or if different games are played at different locations.

2. A small group can meet regularly as a club to participate in a game or games of interest to them.

3. Games can be openly available to residents who wish to play them at any time. A game library can be developed.

4. Games can be taken to residents in their rooms who wish to play alone, with another resident, or with a staff member or a volunteer.

5. Tournaments can be set up for some games.

Games for small groups

To organize games for small groups, the activity director (or other leader) should:

1. Select an appropriate game or games.

2. Review the requirements and rules.

3. Go over the game or games with any staff members, volunteers, or residents who will assist.

4. Get required materials and supplies.

5. Determine the room arrangement in regard to the positioning of tables and chairs.

6. Decide whether prizes will be presented. (If so, they should be made or bought, or donations should be solicited.)

7. Before starting the game, go over the rules briefly with participants.

8. Start playing the game. Verbally guide the participants until all are familiar with the game.

An example of a game suitable for a small group is Bunco (figure 62, page 143).

Quiz programs

In preparation for a quiz program, the activity director should:

1. Select an appropriate quiz game.

2. Review the requirements and rules. Have them written or typed up.

3. If the quiz requires, or would be improved by, outside guests, invite such persons as appropriate a month in advance. In a telephone conversation give the general details of the program, explain their role, and state the purpose of the program. If the person accepts the invitation, get any information needed and indicate that a letter confirming the arrangements will be sent. Some pro-

grams may require more than one contact with the guests prior to their arrival.

4. Review the program with staff members and/or volunteers who will assist. Make such assignments as are necessary, such as scorekeeper, timekeeper, "expert," announcer, and hostess. Assign or assume the responsibility for making up the score sheet or scoreboard (on paper or blackboard); printing name cards; and, when necessary, preparing questions, "sign-in" board, flip cards, floor markings, and making any other preparations that may be needed.

5. Buy, borrow, gather up, or make any materials or supplies that are needed. For example: blackboard and chalk, or materials for another type of scoreboard, eye masks for panelists if a mystery guest is used, bell or horn for timekeepers or "experts," paper, pencils, and prizes.

6. Determine the room arrangement and equipment needed in the way of tables, chairs, podium, microphones, and so forth.

7. Invite or select resident panelists or other resident participants as needed.

8. On the day of the event have a practice session (approximately 30 minutes) with participating residents. Explain how the game is played and the rules that will be followed. Have a mock (practice) session that will be an example for the participants to follow. Sample mimeographed questions should be prepared and given to them to use as guides.

9. Have all equipment and materials arranged prior to starting the quiz.

10. Have all assistants at their assigned positions and ready prior to game time.

During the actual quiz program, the announcer should introduce the activity director or other moderator who then should:

1. Make some opening remarks such as "Good evening, welcome to *(name of nursing home)* version of *(name of quiz)*."

2. Give a history of the game if this information is available, such as what year it was first seen on television, who was the moderator, and so forth.

3. Ask how many in the audience recall the program.

4. Give a summary of how the game is played and the rules. If the audience participates at all, tell them what they will do.

5. Introduce the scorekeeper, timekeeper, or others who will help.

6. Introduce the resident panelists.

7. Begin playing the game. If outside guests or resident guests are involved, introduce them as they are called on (with the exception of any mystery guest that might be scheduled). Keep answers from the panel but show them to the audience. Ask the audience not to whisper or call out the answer. Keep cautioning them.

9. End the game at approximately the time planned. Announce the winner or winners, if any, and present any prizes that were planned.

10. Thank the participants individually. Thank the audience for attending.

On one or more occasions, as an alternative, the answers can be kept from the audience, who can then participate. To do this, a panelist can refer his question to the audience, or the moderator can select someone in the audience to answer, or the moderator can leave it open for anyone to answer. Another alternative is to plan for more panelists than are needed at one time and rotate them.

Suggestions for quiz programs include "Two for the Money" (figure 63, page 144) and "What's My Line?" (figure 64, page 145).

Hobbies

Hobbies involve collecting things, doing things, or learning things. Often, two or all three aspects are inherent in a particular hobby. Many persons spend numerous hours on their avocations. Frequently the interest is based on early life experiences, so it is not unusual to find a person returning to a hobby after recalling pleasures received from it in early life. For others, a void may stimulate the pursuit of a particular pastime.

Individualized special-interest activities are educational as well as recreational. There are really no limits to what a person can select as a hobby. All the activities so far suggested, and all those to follow, can take the form of hobbies. Other possibilities include genealogy, photography, collecting postmarks, and raising tropical fish.

To organize a hobby group, the activity director should first present a general introductory program designed to acquaint residents with the subject by such means as a workshop, lecture, demonstration, exhibit, film, slide presentation, class, or field trip. Residents displaying an interest can be invited to a special follow-up session, where the particular hobby is individually started by all who wish to do so.

Staff or volunteers should then meet individually with the participating residents to further encourage and assist them. It may be helpful to continue the small group sessions weekly or monthly. This permits the residents to discuss their progress and problems with other residents involved in the same activity and also with the staff members or volunteers who are helping.

When the residents develop proficiency, they may provide interesting programs for others and possibly stimulate friends to take up the hobby.

Lectures and Demonstrations

Lectures and demonstrations offer further opportunities for educational programming. Such activities stimulate residents to think about and discuss the topic presented.

It is generally not difficult to recruit a qualified person to voluntarily provide a 45-minute presentation on his specialty. Newspapers provide ideas for persons who might be invited as guest speakers. The activity director should save articles about those who might be contacted in the future.

In addition to the topics listed under Ideas for a Lecture Series (figure 65, page 147), other subjects might be of interest to the residents. There may also be value in offering lectures on the psychological, biological, and physical aspects of aging.

The lecture or demonstration can be made effective by following these points made by Plotnick and Shaw.[5]

1. If the speaker is to speak in a room or hall other than an auditorium, it is a good rule of thumb that fewer chairs than might be needed should be set up. If attendance is greater, additional chairs can be brought in.

2. Experience has shown that an audience's response to the speaker's lecture is enhanced if the speaker holds forth from an empty platform. It is best if the person making the introduction leaves the stage after his remarks.

3. The host who introduces the speaker should limit his remarks to two to four minutes.

4. The speaker should be asked to prepare a lecture of about 40 minutes. A longer presentation, even if it is of excellent quality and even if it seems that the audience can "take it," will cut down on the amount of time available for question-and-answer periods and, if the speaker is a celebrity, autograph signing.

5. It is good policy to check with the speaker about taping the speech. Also, it is a good idea to discourage the taking of photographs (especially with flash bulbs) during the lecture.

6. The question-and-answer session should last as long as it can be carried on at a high level of interest and stimulation. A good rule of thumb is 10 to 15 minutes. But always keep in mind that it is far better for the audience to leave "wanting more" than to leave feeling that the evening was just a "bit too long."

7. Often a speaker will prefer to handle the question-and-answer session himself. If, however, he indicates that he would prefer to have someone else manage the session, this person should be prepared to take over the meeting immediately and get right into the questions and answers.

8. As with radio and television "talk shows," it is a good idea to have one or two "plants" in the audience. The plant is especially useful here in getting the question-and-answer session going, because most people are reticent about asking the first question.

To organize and conduct a lecture or demonstration, the activity director (or other leader) should:

1. Develop a file of interesting groups and individuals. Jot down on 3-inch by 5-inch cards the name of the person to contact and his telephone number and address. Indicate the specific skill or talent the person or persons have, and note the reference for obtaining this information. Add any additional comments that might be helpful.

2. Consider the time and the date the program should be offered. Be prepared with one or two alternative dates in case the preferred date is unacceptable to the contact.

[5]Plotnick, M., and Shaw, E. Using guest speakers. *Adult Leadership.* 18:111, Oct. 1969.

3. Call the contact person approximately a month to two weeks in advance of the time the program is planned. After a short introduction, briefly describe the program and its purpose, and then invite the individual to be your guest, suggesting the date previously selected. If the person accepts the invitation, give additional information as to the time of the program, location of the nursing home, and the location in which the performance will be given. If the person needs equipment, such as a slide projector, table, or podium, tell him what is available. Thank the person, and tell him that he will receive a letter confirming the arrangements.

4. Approximately a week prior to the program, send the confirmation letter. Reaffirm the telephone arrangements, giving the who, what, when, where, and why.

5. Prepare the area for the event prior to the program.

6. Make the final announcement of the activity to the residents one-half to one hour prior to starting, depending on how long it will take to get the residents to the area where the activity will be held.

7. Anticipate the arrival of the guest, and be prepared to personally greet him and go over any final arrangements. Take his hat, coat, and so forth. Assist with any equipment brought for the purpose.

8. With interest and enthusiasm, introduce the person or group to the audience.

9. Display interest by sitting with the residents and being attentive to the presentation. At the end of the program, allow a few minutes for questions.

10. After the activity, thank the lecturer on behalf of the entire audience.

11. Thank the guest personally after he has finished or is about to leave. Offer to help carry out any equipment brought along for use in the program.

12. A day or two later, send the guest a thank-you letter or note expressing appreciation. Make the note unique and personal whenever possible. If he might be invited back, indicate that the residents look forward to his return. Good public relations is the key to success in this kind of effort.

Literature

Creative writing, prose or verse, is an area that many people seem to think is reserved for a select group of professionals. This is not true, and an activity director passing over this subject because of a lack of personal interest not only will stunt the activity program but also will do an injustice to the residents. Imaginative writing offers an outlet for expressing one's feelings or telling of one's experiences. The challenge is to motivate residents to "write it down." Projects or classes on creative writing can be included on a group or individual basis. Probably the best way that the activity director can encourage a resident to write is to approach him individually, at appropriate times when he would be likely to respond favorably, and suggest that he write down a particular thing.

Many residents enjoy reading other persons' writings, whether prose or poetry, fiction or nonfiction. Books and magazines should be available to the residents. A call to organizations within the community will most often result in a large donation of books. Current magazines can often be received free of charge by contacting the local post office and requesting magazines that cannot be delivered for one reason or another. If the request is granted, the post office will most likely ask that someone come to its headquarters to pick them up.

Through such means as suggested here, a nursing home could begin its own library if space is available. Otherwise, a bookshelf, book rack, book cart, or even bookends can be utilized. Magazines can be placed in a rack or on tables. Plays, dramatic readings, and poetry that have been recorded may be available in the public library. Books can also be borrowed from the library. In a community with a bookmobile, it is possible that the activity director could arrange for the bookmobile to visit on a regular or periodic basis. For the resident whose vision is poor, large-print reading material may be necessary.

Whatever method is used for making books available to the residents, it is important that residents' interest in reading be stimulated. Bedridden residents should have the same opportunities as ambulatory residents for selecting reading material. Group readings, led preferably by a resident or, if this is not possible, by a staff member or volunteer, may encourage individuals to pick up a book by themselves.

Book reviews presented by residents can also be arranged. Or book reviews, play reviews, and poetry or dramatic readings can be presented by guests. Librarians, teachers, and women's club members are possible sources.

To encourage residents to use the library, books that are available can be publicized by displaying posters and exhibits near the library or by holding cultural activities in the library. Having a resident serve as the librarian may be helpful to that resident as well as to others. Earl Nightengale, in his film *The Strangest Secret,* said, "If you want to hide something from the American Public, put it in the library." The activity director should not let this be true in the nursing home.

To organize book reading programs for small groups, the activity director (or other leader) should:

1. Select appropriate and interesting reading material in advance. It may be a short piece that is readable in a half hour to an hour, or a longer reading (such as a novel) that would be continued over several meetings.
2. Prepare the setting so it is conducive to an informal gathering. A table may or may not be used, depending upon what is most comfortable. Arranging the group in a circle commands their attention. Good lighting is essential. A microphone is advisable if some residents have hearing difficulties. Plan visual aids if they are to be used.
3. Welcome each resident at the beginning of the program. If necessary, help residents to be seated and arrange wheelchairs.
4. Introduce the material that will be read. If a book is being continued, give a brief review. If possible, have one or more in the group give the review.
5. Begin reading. Read slowly, and enunciate clearly. Keep the best possible eye contact with the group. When appropriate, pause at periodic intervals in order to discuss what is going on in the book, allow comments, or ask about an unfamiliar pronunciation. This permits residents to share information with one another and the leader.
6. End the reading near the scheduled time, and thank the residents for participating. Announce when the next reading program will be held.

To vary the reading program, the leader might encourage a particular resident to read, rotate reading among several residents, or possibly ask a different resident to read at each session. Other alternatives are to present only a review of the book or to ask a resident to read and report on a book of his choosing.

Music

Music can be conveyed by voice or instrument. It can be participated in by one (solo), two (duet), three (trio), four (quartet), or large groups. It can be formal or informal. Musical tastes vary. Different residents may prefer popular, classical, operatic, country-western, or religious music.

Community singing to the "old standards" probably appeals to the majority. Song sheets, preferably in large print, should be given to each person; when possible, slides can be used. Group singing is most successful when there is piano accompaniment. Recorded accompaniment is possible but less desirable.

Residents who would like to sing solo or with a small select group, such as a barbershop quartet, should be encouraged to practice and periodically perform at various events. An ensemble, choir, chorus, groups of chamber singers, or glee club can be developed among resident groups.

Residents capable of playing instruments should be encouraged to do so. Bands, orchestras, or ensembles can be organized when there are enough musicians. Instruction classes might be planned for beginners or intermediates. Rhythm bands or kitchen bands can offer a lot of fun for participants. Bell-ringing groups can be started.

Musical programs involving residents may result in more than the immediate enjoyment if the vocal or instrumental talent is used to highlight other activities. Examples include the use of special music in worship services; performances in talent nights, at parties, and at special events such as open house; involvement in dramatic programs and pageants; the production of concerts; and organizing a Christmas caroling group to perform outside the nursing home.

The examples that are listed above are also excellent spectator activities. In the absence of such resident talent, staff members or volunteers can be asked to perform. Record listening, possibly with commentary by a disc jockey (a professional, a resident, or a volunteer) can be planned as a program in itself or incorporated with a dance. Some nursing homes have automatic piped-in (taped) music.

Occasionally, individuals call the institution and ask to perform. Even so, the activity director will most often need to make initial contact with individuals and organizations in the community. Sources to investigate for various types of musical programs are churches, public and private schools and colleges, clubs, groups such as symphony orchestras and music leagues, nearby military bases, sororities and fraternities, professional musicians' unions, prisons, business and industrial firms, music schools, and individuals known in the community or publicized by the media.

Other possibilities for resident participation include music appreciation classes (see Educational Classes, page 109), physical exercises to music (see Exercise, page 111), and musical games (see Games, page 112).

To organize a group singing program, the activity director (or other leader) should:

1. Select with residents the types of songs they enjoy, and determine some specific favorites. Generally keep the songs familiar to the residents, and not too fast and not too draggy.
2. Find songbooks that contain the selected music. If it is not feasible to buy a songbook for each person, type up the songs to be used on a ditto or mimeograph stencil and run off the number of copies needed.
3. Seek a resident or volunteer who will play the piano for the sing-a-long.
4. Ask a resident, volunteer, or staff member to lead the singing.
5. Ask the piano player to play while the residents are entering the area.
6. Ask the song leader to indicate the title of each song and where it can be found.
7. If the audience has access to other songs in their books, encourage them to request or suggest a number or two.

If the nursing home has a slide projector, 15 to 25 selected songs can be photographed and made into slides. When shown on a screen, the slides can be easily seen by the audience. If an overhead projector is available, sheet music or typed copies of the selections can be projected on a screen and again seen easily.

Nature and Outdoor Activities

Although gardening is probably the most common nature activity conducted in nursing homes, other natural phenomena can also stimulate the appreciation and interest of residents. Some activities are appropriate for indoors; others are more desirable or only possible outdoors.

In addition to indoor and outdoor gardening (figures 66 and 67, pages 150 and 151), other activities include floral arranging; weather forecasting; astronomy; caring for birds, animals, and fish; collecting specimens of leaves, flowers, rocks, and shells; bird-watching; lapidary work; using nature objects in craft projects; fishing; cookouts; and day camps. Those who can assist in determining other possibilities include forest rangers (naturalists); garden clubs; archaeological societies; Audubon and wildlife clubs; astronomy clubs; university extension centers; museums and academies of science; conservation clubs; nature clubs; and groups interested in geology and fossils, such as lapidary clubs, gem and mineral societies, and rock clubs.

Lectures, demonstrations, exhibits, classes, and workshops can be arranged with the aid of the sources mentioned. Movies and slides are available on many related subjects. Field trips can be scheduled to parks, botanical gardens, greenhouses, nature centers, and zoos. Drives in the country or walks in the park also foster appreciation for the natural environment.

Nature projects can be individual or group programs. They can be carried out very informally. For example, residents can care for plants in their rooms, or they can work alone on a project such as building a birdhouse.

To organize nature groups, the activity director (or other leader) should:

1. Determine the interests of residents.
2. Meet with knowledgeable persons concerning the activity selected. Survey community resources.
3. Decide upon the types of projects or activities that would be interesting, enjoyable, and within the capabilities of the residents. Consider the time limit of the project(s).
4. Purchase or request donations of any equipment and supplies needed in order to begin.
5. Make arrangements that permit involvement by all who are interested.

6. Introduce the project to the residents, explaining what will be done as a group and how they can take part individually.

7. If necessary, give a brief demonstration of what they are to do.

8. Permit the residents to begin. Be available for assistance and guidance.

9. Allow the residents to help clean up, if cleanup is necessary.

10. Conclude the program at an appropriate time.

To expand on a nature project, the activity director should think of how those not participating can benefit from the efforts of the group. In gardening, the plants can be displayed or donated to others. In weather forecasting, data can be presented daily to all residents. In collecting things or making things, an exhibit can be held. Such methods can encourage others to participate.

Outings and Trips

The value of outings to the residents should not be overlooked. Trips are helpful in providing information and understanding, maintaining appreciation of the environment and the arts, and offering other refreshing benefits to those generally confined to a limited physical environment. Activities in the community not only provide a needed change for the residents but also stimulate a renewal of interests.

Trips to all sorts of places are possible. Examples of places to go and things to do in the community have been mentioned in other sections of this chapter. The residents who are capable of making the trips should be involved in the decisions as to where to go. They may decide to go to a show, attend a sports event, take a tour, visit a nightclub, arrange a picnic, go shopping, or whatever. If possible, they should take at least one trip each month.

Admission. Many things can be done when there is no admission charge, but when there is a normal charge, the activity director often can make advance arrangements to have residents and supervisory personnel admitted at no cost. A letter sent to the ticket manager requesting complimentary admission to an event will generally produce the desired results (figure 33, page 48). In most instances, the letter should be mailed at least a month in advance. If the request cannot be allowed, the activity director can attempt to receive a reduced rate and have residents pay their own admission. In this case, the nursing home should assume the cost of admission for supervisory staff and volunteers.

Advance arrangements. The activity director should not take residents anywhere without having first evaluated the conditions. The site should be visited in advance. Factors to consider include: steps, location of restrooms, parking arrangements, size of elevators, problems in unloading and loading of vehicles, fire exits, location of seats, best route, temperature and climate, refreshments, ticket window, entrance, safety hazards, size of crowd, time to arrive and leave, and tour guides.

Transportation and insurance. The number of facilities having their own courtesy cars or buses is few, and most nursing homes must look elsewhere for transportation. Chartering a bus is expensive, so other possibilities should be considered. An American Red Cross motor pool in the area might be of help. Possibly a school or industry would provide a bus; in this case it may be necessary to pay the driver regular wages or partial wages. If nothing else materializes, possibly a staff member or volunteer can provide the necessary transportation. Whatever approach is taken, it is imperative that the nursing home have proper and adequate liability insurance coverage. The administrator should consult with the institution's lawyer and insurance representative to find out what is needed.

Medical approval. The list of residents who wish to go on a trip should be screened by the nursing director. The nursing director, in turn, should contact each resident's physician. The physician should be responsible for granting approval and indicating any special precautions (figure 17, page 31).

Safety precautions. The safety of residents from departure to return is certainly a big responsibility. This should not, however, deter the nursing home from scheduling trips, but should emphasize the need for using sound judgment and taking proper steps to avoid risks. Residents confined to wheelchairs should be fastened to their chairs by wheelchair safety straps throughout the trip, wheel locks should be functional, and handle grips should be tight. Precautions should be taken to ensure safety in loading and unloading. When the vehicle is moving, the wheelchair should be locked and the wheels blocked to eliminate rolling and sliding.

Whoever is pushing the chair should know how to manipulate it.

Residents capable of transferring from wheelchair to automobile should be assisted by a staff member trained in the proper methods of transferring. This training could be done by a registered occupational therapist or a physical therapist. The wheelchairs can be folded and placed in the trunk if the residents will be getting out of the vehicle.

Residents who are able to walk without assistance or who can use canes or walkers should be supervised and have assistance available to them if needed.

Parties

Parties can be planned to celebrate many events. Birthdays are very personal, and each resident should receive birthday wishes on his day. In small institutions, a party can be planned for each resident's birthday, but larger institutions can select one date each month for a large birthday party recognizing all residents with birthdays in that month. Inviting the closest relatives of each birthday person should be considered.

Married residents may wish to celebrate their wedding anniversary. Residents may wish to arrange special events for personnel, such as retirement, going away, and housewarming parties; bridal and baby showers; and wedding receptions.

Cocktail parties or cocktail hours are held regularly in some nursing homes.

Parties can express the spirit of such holidays as New Year's Day, Valentine's Day, April Fool's Day, St. Patrick's Day, Halloween, Mardi Gras, or Christmas. They can be held to recognize historical or patriotic events, such as Lincoln's Birthday, Washington's Birthday, Memorial Day, Flag Day Independence Day, Labor Day, Columbus Day, or Veterans Day. Changing seasons offer more themes for parties.

A welcome tea/coffee for new residents can be very valuable in getting new people acquainted during their early adjustment period. In addition to socializing and having refreshments, this is a time for the new arrivals to be introduced to the services and activities available to them. These programs can be scheduled periodically, depending on the turnover rate in the facility. The residents' welcome committee can be charged with this responsibility.

In order to efficiently organize the parties, it is advisable to outline the program in the manner suggested by the Checklist for Organizing a Birthday Party (figure 68, page 152). Whatever theme is selected, it should be followed throughout the games, entertainment, decorations, and refreshments.

Service Projects

Charitable and volunteer activities that involve direct resident participation include community services and nursing home services. Individual residents may be capable of contributing money, time, and skill, or a group of residents may accept a particular project or projects.

In the area of community services, residents can:
• Contribute to health funds.
• Donate craft items.
• Assume financial adoption of a child, or assist in sending supplies.
• Contribute to CARE.
• Sew dressings or other items for the American Cancer Society.
• Make or mend toys for children.
• Knit articles for displaced persons.
• Cook or bake for community organizations, church affairs, the USO, and so forth.
• Tutor children and adults.
• Send magazines to shut-ins.
• Provide telephone reassurance to shut-ins.
• Raise plants for distribution to the sick.
• Provide entertainment to hospitalized, homebound, those at a convent, and so forth.
• Serve as substitute grandparents for children.
• Stuff envelopes or kits for mailing.

In the nursing home itself, residents can perform useful services. Depending upon individual capabilities, residents can:
• Deliver mail.
• Water plants and arrange flowers.
• Serve as a receptionist.
• Visit other residents.
• Make arts or crafts samples for display.
• Set tables.
• Mend clothes and sew on buttons.
• Assist in the gift shop.
• Work as a librarian, or arrange magazines if there is no library.
• Lead group singing or group reading.

- Write personalized verses for residents' birthday cards.
- Teach Sunday School.
- Run the motion picture projector, slide projector, or record player.
- Teach a skill.
- Assist in preparation and cleanup.
- Do gift wrapping.

For group projects, everyone can do the same thing, each can work on something different, or several can be assigned to a part of the project. Residents can work on a project during their leisure time, or after volunteering to help they can be assigned a time to do a certain service.

To organize specific service projects for small groups of residents, the activity director (or other leader) should:

1. Survey the needs of the nursing home and the community. Prepare a list of possible service projects that residents are capable of doing, and present it to the residents. Let the residents decide what project or projects they would like to help with.
2. Make any necessary arrangements with the departments within the nursing home or with the persons or organizations that will be assisted.
3. Arrange for and obtain any necessary supplies or equipment.
4. Arrange the time and the place for the project.
5. When the project begins, tell each resident about his responsibility, and provide instructions and any necessary supplies.
6. Supervise until the group is familiar with the task. If necessary, be available at all times.

Special Events

Activities that are especially enjoyable, intriguing, and looked forward to by the residents can be called special events. Included are such activities as a bazaar, picnic, open house, or extravaganza. An annual event, or an activity sponsored only once, also can be classified as a special event. Possibly the entire institution, including all departments, can work together to arrange such programs as a country fair, Olympic games, carnival, Las Vegas extravaganza, kite day, or any other special offering.

Imagination is the key; preferably the activity director and the residents should develop their own, unique special events, such as a fashion show (figure 69, page 153), watermelon feast (figure 70, page 153), or picnic (figure 71, page 154).

To organize a special event, the activity director (or other leader) should:

1. Determine with the residents far in advance what special event is to be planned, and set a date.
2. Begin developing the plans. Make arrangements for the area to be used.
3. Schedule the staff or volunteers who will be required, and keep them up to date on the plans.
4. Coordinate with other services or departments to receive full cooperation.
5. Write up the activity or activities, listing tasks to be done and supplies to be obtained. Make the necessary preparations.
6. Schedule any people or groups who will be a part of the program.
7. Select and order any refreshments desired. Think of diabetics and others on special diets.
8. Publicize the coming activity to residents and possibly to their families and friends. Arrange to have a guest register, if desired.
9. Make any necessary purchases, rentals, or borrowings.
10. Do any decorating or building that is scheduled.
11. Make all last-minute preparations.
12. At the beginning of the event, welcome residents and guests and start the program.
13. Follow through on the plans.

Sports

Sports receive considerable attention from the American public, but opportunities for sports participation for the elderly are limited. However, when necessary, some activities can be adapted for residents by such means as altering the rules or adjusting the devices used. The following are some examples of various ways to adapt sports for participation by residents, even those confined to wheelchairs.

Archery. Use lightweight bows and arrows with rubber suction tips.

Bowling. Use an indoor plastic set. At a commercial bowling alley, use a special ball.

Croquet. Use a lightweight set and larger wickets. Some residents may be capable of using a regulation set.

Darts. Use rubber suction darts.

Golf. Use an indoor putting set with lightweight putters.

Horseshoes. Use a rubber indoor set at close distance; this can also be played outdoors. Some residents may be able to use a regular set at shorter-than-regulation distance.

Quoits. Use a lightweight set with five pegs.

Shuffleboard. Use lightweight cues and discs with a shortened playing area and larger dimensions for the landing area.

Volleyball. Lower the net, use a balloon as the volleyball, and decrease the playing area. More than one ball can be used at the same time.

Some residents may be capable of playing billiards or ping-pong. Others may like to practice casting or go on a fishing trip.

Spectator activities will no doubt interest many residents. Such activities include baseball, basketball, football, ice hockey, auto or horse or boat racing, boxing, wrestling, archery, track and field, tennis, soccer, gymnastics, and swimming and diving. The activity staff should find out what activities the residents would enjoy attending and then plan outings to professional events or to those sponsored by high schools, colleges, country clubs, the YMCA, or the city recreation department.

The activity staff can arrange demonstrations by various athletic individuals or organizations for such activities as fencing, soccer, gymnastics, judo, ping-pong, and billiards. If a demonstration requires equipment that is not available, such as a ping-pong table, the activity staff might be able to borrow the item from a local community center, recreation department of a school, YMCA, or club.

Lectures by professional athletes are sometimes obtainable in a metropolitan area by contacting the speakers' bureau of the professional team. Free films on sports are available from many sources.

To organize sports programs for small groups, the activity director (or other leader) should:

1. Select the appropriate activity or activities.
2. Review the requirements and rules. Make necessary adaptations.
3. Go over the activity with any staff members, volunteers, or residents who will assist.
4. Get supplies or equipment that will be needed.
5. Determine the most suitable room arrangement.
6. At the beginning of the program, explain the rules and demonstrate the procedures.

Many variations of the basic sports program can be planned. For example, more than one event can be planned for the period if games can be completed in a short time or if different events are played at different locations. A small group can meet regularly, almost as a club, to participate in a game or games of interest. Tournaments can be planned. Pyramid and ladder tournaments can take place over a long period of time. Single-elimination and double-elimination tournaments can be scheduled for shorter time periods. Special sports programs, such as Olympic games, can be planned.

Directions for organizing specific sports activities are included for reference (figures 72 through 76, pages 155 through 157).

Visitation Programs

Certainly many residents have a need for interaction with others that goes beyond what staff can provide. However, staff members are definitely an integral part of this broader person-to-person program. The staff should encourage family and friends to visit and even to attend activities with the resident. Arrangements should be possible whereby they can be invited to a meal occasionally. Volunteers can be assigned as friendly visitors or, with additional training, can become "companionship therapists" (figure 39b, page 68). In many cases residents can visit other residents, just as neighbors visit other neighbors.

Clergymen should be notified when members of their congregation are admitted to the nursing home (figure 77, page 158). The clergymen and the members of the congregation should be welcome to visit.

Nursing homes having contacts with Veterans Administration hospitals should contact the VA chief of voluntary service to inquire about "The Patient Returns to the Community" program.

Worship Services

The opportunity to worship as part of the regularly scheduled activities is spiritually therapeutic to residents. In all forms of religious activity residents can experience a closeness to God as the creator and sustainer of life. As in other forms of fellowship, worship services offer the sustaining effect of sharing this experience with others of like mind. There is value, too, in the participation of the individual. Certainly the mind benefits wherever there is clearer insight and understanding of God, of religion, and of life itself.

Although worship may not include a monetary offering, there is always the beneficial sense of personal stewardship derived from the giving of time and support to the worship activity. In common prayer the needs and the hopes of all in the group can be expressed with a power different from that of individual prayer. Through the sermon or meditation may come the education, inspiration, or dedication that has a sustaining effect for the residents and may provide all-important meaning and motivation to the life effort. Worship is by no means the only religious activity possible, but it is primary and basic as one of the activities that support people in their daily lives.

The activity director should get a list of residents of each faith, and those who wish to attend services should be assisted in doing so.

Arrangements can be made with local churches and synagogues to provide clergymen to conduct services. The clergymen may wish to visit ill residents who could not attend. If a clergyman is not available to conduct the service, a lay person can be recruited. Or a capable resident can be asked to give a brief sermon mixed with song and prayer.

The service should generally be limited to one hour. It can be held in a chapel if available; otherwise, an auditorium, lounge, day room, or other area will suffice. Residents with hearing difficulties would benefit from a public address system if one is available. A podium would be the only other necessary item.

Special music, vocal and/or instrumental, may be a part of the service. Music can be planned by the nursing home or the clergyman. A volunteer or resident pianist will be useful during the singing of hymns. The clergyman may serve as the song leader, or he may provide one. Otherwise a volunteer or resident should be asked to be responsible.

Prayerbooks, songbooks, and Bibles can be, and usually are, supplied by the nursing home. If it is not possible for the home to buy these books,

churches and synagogues in the area should be informed of the need, and they may be able to donate the books.

Bible study, Sunday School classes, prayer meetings, and hymn sings can be organized in addition to the regular services. These programs can be conducted by an employee, a resident, or a volunteer.

If a duplicating machine is available, it can be used to duplicate a program that gives the order of worship and announces any forthcoming religious programs.

Religious holidays should not be overlooked when schedules are being developed. Often, national holidays are recognized in the regular worship services. National Brotherhood Week and World Day of Prayer provide other times for spiritual reflection and personal evaluation.

Catholic services

Nursing homes having residents of the Catholic faith will ordinarily be cared for by the priest of the neighborhood parish. Where this is not the case, the diocesan chancery office should be contacted to arrange for a priest. In places where a priest's availability of time is limited, a deacon may conduct a communion service or, in some places, a layman designated as an extraordinary minister of communion may conduct the service.

Ideally, Mass, or at least a communion service, should take place on Sunday. If this is not feasible, it will have to take place on a weekday. Whoever will conduct the service should be contacted ahead of time to see what physical arrangements need to be made.

Simple prayers or Bible services may be conducted by anyone, clerical or lay.

Whenever a resident suffers from a serious illness or the weakness of old age, he may receive Anointing of the Sick. This is not to be viewed as "last rites" for someone who is dying, but rather the official prayer and sacrament of the Catholic Church for the restoration of health. It may be administered only by a priest, who should be notified as soon as a resident's condition becomes serious. The Sacrament of Anointing also may be administered communally to a group of residents either during Mass or at a special service.

The Sacrament of Reconciliation (Confession) should be available on a regular basis to all residents who request it. It is administered only by a priest and may take place privately or in the context of a communal service during which individual confessions will be heard. If a resident should become in danger of death, it is most important that he receive this sacrament, if at all possible.

The sacrament for the dying is Viaticum (Holy Communion). Whenever a resident's condition becomes critical (in danger of death), the priest should be notified immediately, day or night, and informed of the person's condition, namely, whether or not the Anointing of the Sick had been previously administered, whether he is conscious and able to make a confession, and whether he is able to swallow at least a small particle of the host given in Communion.

Jewish services

Jewish services that can adequately serve all branches of Judaism require the leader of a service to be knowledgeable in the Hebrew language and the proper order of the service. In the absence of such a person, selected prayers from the prayerbook can be recited by individuals separately or as part of a group. The order of the service is found in the section of the prayerbook dealing with each particular service.

Specific prayers are designated for daily, Sabbath, and holiday worship. Morning services can be held from sunrise until 11 a.m. Afternoon services are recited from 1 p.m. until sunset. Evening services take place from 20 minutes after sunset until sunrise the following day.

The Sabbath is an important weekly occasion. A typical service can be presented on Friday evening at the beginning of the Sabbath, and/or a Saturday morning service can be conducted. It is permissible for lay Jews to conduct services, so if a rabbi is not available, employees, volunteers, or residents could do so.

In addition to the services, Jewish women light candles every Friday afternoon and before holidays in order to usher in the Sabbath or holiday. Sacramental wine is used in the recitation of prayers relating to both the Sabbath and holidays.

At the table where the Sabbath or holiday meal is eaten, sacramental wine and two Sabbath loaves are provided on the eve of the Sabbath and holiday. On Saturday and holiday mornings, after services, sacramental wine and refreshments are served. At the midday meals, two Sabbath loaves are provided.

Protestant services

Services for residents of any of the Protestant denominations should be held each week, preferably on Sunday. The major task is to obtain a minister for each of these services. It may be that one particular minister will accept responsibility to regularly provide the church services. Possibly a ministerial alliance or association in the area will aid by scheduling ministers on a rotating basis. In any case, an alternate or substitute should always be available in case of cancellations.

If desired, an offering can be collected. The money received could go for various Christian purposes, inside or outside the nursing home.

Communion services should be established on a regular basis for those who wish to take part. An open communion is advisable at least quarterly, so that all residents who wish to participate in the observance may do so. The day of World Wide Communion is an ideal time to schedule a communion service.

A communion service would involve arranging for the necessary materials. Either the minister and his church or the nursing home would need to provide small pieces of bread or crackers, a serving plate, wine (usually grape juice), and small glasses or paper cups.

figure 47
list of materials
for craft products

MATERIALS FOR CRAFT PRODUCTS

Material	Process	Products
Copper	Tooling	Pictures
		Bookends
	Enameling	Ashtrays
		Jewelry
		Bowls
		Coasters
Silver	Smithing	Jewelry
		Buckles
Leather	Lacing	Moccasins
		Purses
		Cases
		Belts
	Tooling	Albums
		Purses
		Cases
Wood	Finishing	Stools
	Building	Jewelry cases
	Burning	Trays
	Whittling	Pictures
	Chipping	Figures
	Carving	Boxes
		Designs
Cork		Coasters
		Hot plates
Clay	Casting	Plaques
		Chess pieces
	Modeling	Statues
		Imaginative items
Gravel (mosaic)		Pictures
		Folding screens
Seeds (mosaic)	Designing	Pictures
Wax	Molding	Candles (rolled or formed)
Sponge	Cutting	Bath toys

**figure 47
(cont.)**

Material	Process	Products
Shells		Jewelry Pictures Soap dishes
Feathers		Dusters Floral arrangements
Raffia	Weaving	Baskets Mats
	Winding	Bottles Wire-framed animals
Reed	Weaving	Baskets Mats Bowls
Wire	Sculpting	Abstract figures Mobiles Jewelry
Foam rubber	Covering	Lint dusters Covered hangers
Glass	Designing	Lampshades Bowls Mobiles
	Etching	Monogrammed drinking glasses
	Heating	Ashtrays
Paper	Folding magazine	Figures Centerpieces Decorations
	Rolling magazine	Wastepaper cans Baskets
	Quilling	Pictures Plaques
	Mâché-pasting	Masks Candle holders Ornaments
	Origami (folding) Tissue paper	Decorations Greeting cards Stained glass Flowers

**figure 47
(cont.)**

Material	Process	Products
Paper (cont.)	Crepe paper	Flowers Decorations
	Decoupage	Wall hangings Cases Wastepaper cans
Plastic cellulose	Tying	Hangers Wreaths
liquid	Casting	Centerpieces Lamps
jugs	Decorating	Animal centerpieces
Plaster	Casting	Plaques Jewelry Ornaments
Soap	Carving	Figures
Styrofoam		Decorations Table pieces
String	Weaving	Coasters Mats Belts Straps
	Knotting	Thick and thin
Chenille/pipe cleaners	Bending	Corsages Table decorations Stick figures
Felt	Cutting and designing	Decorations Puppets Stuffed articles
	Collage	Pictures Coverings for boxes Cans
Yarn	Weaving	Place mats Runners Bags
Yarn (cont.)	Knitting Hooking	Clothing Rugs Wall hangings
	Winding Knotting	Yarn dolls Tufted rugs

**figure 47
(cont.)**

Material	Process	Products
Nylon net	Cutting and tying	Covers Clothes hangers Decorations Soap bars Lint dusters
Burlap	Raveling (pasting, cutting)	Wall hangings Flowers Handbags Yardstick holders Bulletin boards Wreaths
Ribbon	Tying	Flowers Bows Corsages Finishing touches
Tile (mosaic)	Designing	Ashtrays Trivets Pictures Bowls Jewelry boxes
Rags	Braiding Draping	Rugs Dolls Figures for decorations Centerpieces

**figure 48
checklist for
copper tooling**

CHECKLIST FOR COPPER TOOLING

Materials

Wooden forming tools
Copper (or aluminum) sheeting
Masking tape
Plaster of paris, clay, or wax
Designs
Liver of sulfur
Frames or plyboard
Sealing lacquer
Template (for Method 2)

Steps: Method 1

1. Put a magazine or pad under the work to give a softer surface. Cover sharp edges of metal with masking tape.
2. Tape design to metal sheet.
3. Transfer design onto metal using pencil or stylus.
4. Turn metal to other (back) side. With stylus, retrace outline only; stay just inside first outline (about 1/32 of an inch).
5. With the back side still up, raise the inside of design by pressing gently with tools. It may be necessary to place a very soft pad under the work to push the metal.
6. Turn to front. With spatula, press background. This erases original line of design.
7. Fill in mold with plaster of paris, clay, or wax.

Steps: Method 2

1. Cut copper tooling to size of template; tape with masking tape on four sides.
2. Press out design with rounded edge of modeling tool.
3. To tool, press out details with pointed end.
4. Remove copper from template; fill in impression with clay.

Coloring or antiquing

1. Prepare liver of sulfur solution. Strong solution will make darker, more definite color.
2. Apply evenly to metal with cloth dabbed in solution.
   When antique color desired is reached, put metal under water to wash off, thereby stopping oxidation of metal.
3. Rub dried metal surface with steel wool for highlighting.
4. Seal surface by painting with clear metal lacquer.

Mounting or framing

Project can be framed as a picture, used to decorate a box or bookends, and so forth.
For picture: Frame in regular way; use 1/4-inch plyboard, one inch larger than picture, sanded and finished; tack picture to wood with escutcheon pins (small gold tacks).
For decoration: Attach to (wood) box with escutcheon pins.

Skills

Skills required include one-handed use of pencil and small tools, good eyesight, and fair mental alertness.

figure 49
checklist for
decoupage

CHECKLIST FOR DECOUPAGE

Materials

Picture	Stain	Picture hanger
Board	Brush	Decoupage sealer
Sandpaper	Glue	Decoupage varnish
File		

Steps

1. Determine if picture is to have straight or irregular sides. If straight, four sides must be extended out on edges. This is accomplished with light strokes, from inside out, with a No. 100 Grit sandpaper. If picture is to be irregular in shape, determine outline, then tear in a downward motion.
2. Select board. Board should be of a size to give a margin on all four sides of picture; the usual thickness is ½ inch.
3. Decide whether to distress board on edges. If so, this is accomplished by knife, file, or electric sanding discs. Files are preferred because there is little chance for injury.
4. Decide if color (pigment) or stain is to be used on margin. If so, this must be done before mounting of picture. These decisions depend on the type of wood used and color or finish desired.
5. Use decoupage sealer over the whole board.
6. Mount the picture.
   a. Spray the back with decoupage sealer to prevent absorption of the glue into the picture.
   b. Cover the back of the picture with a diluted solution of glue (1 teaspoon water and 1 ounce glue). Apply solution to board, making all margins equal.
   c. In applying picture, use a roller to roll out all excess glue and all air bubbles. Roll from center to the outer edge. Wipe off glue from roller after each stroke. Permit to dry overnight.
7. The treatment of decoupage is generally done with a product known as "Spun Magic." Apply it with a 1½-inch brush. After the complete surface has been coated, keep drying the brush and the stroke surface to eliminate surplus material. This coating process is to be completed at least 10 times, with each coat at right angles to the preceding coat.
8. Sand the picture. The first sanding process should be done with a No. 320 Grit Wet or Dry sandpaper, used on a padded block. Sanding should be done until quite smooth; however, care should be taken not to sand through decoupage and onto picture.
9. Apply two more coats of "Spun Magic," allow to dry, and repeat the sanding process. Continue until desired depth and smoothness of finish is obtained. This may take up to 20 coats of material and sanding. Finish with No. 400 Grit sandpaper for a smoother surface.
10. Apply a good quality hard wax to give the completed project a fine gloss. If a dull finish is desired, rub lightly with a "0000" grade of steel wool.
11. To hang the picture, use a "saw tooth" and an ornamental screw in the loop on the top edge.

figure 50
checklist for making
gravel mosaic pictures

CHECKLIST FOR MAKING GRAVEL MOSAIC PICTURES

Materials

Gravel (or something similar, such as beans, shells, seeds)
Braid or cord for outline
Glue
Backing (plywood, masonite, cardboard with burlap covering)
Frame (optional, can be baseboard molding on two sides of picture)
Design
Newspaper (to protect working surface)

Steps

1. Prepare board or backing.
2. Choose design; also decide on color scheme. Choose a design that can be sectioned into areas for gravel of different colors. Designs can be purchased at craft shops. For an original design, it is advisable to experiment with graveling and colors first. Not all designs are suitable for mosaics.
3. Transfer design to backing.
4. Glue braid, outlining and sectioning the design. Black braid is used most often.
5. Apply glue and gravel. Apply thin coat of glue to areas designed for one color. Sprinkle gravel to cover glued area. Let stand for a few minutes; then tilt board to shake off excess gravel. Check that area is completely covered with gravel before going on to another color. Beans, shells, and larger objects are usually placed individually and can give the effect of direction—for example, feathers on a bird.

Products

Although pictures and various wall hangings are usually produced, other products include decoration for cornices, wood jewel boxes, and tabletops.

Applications

This craft can be an individual or a group project. In doing several pictures at one time, some persons can sand boards while others assemble pictures.

Skills

Although preparation of the backing and sprinkling of gravel do not require good hand coordination, the braid work, glue spreading, and design transfer demand dexterity.

**figure 51
checklist for
leather lacing**

CHECKLIST FOR LEATHER LACING

Materials

Leather kit
Lace
Needles
Glue (all-purpose glue or special glue for leather)
Awl

Steps

1. Thread needle. Put glue on end of thread, attach to needle, and clamp in vise for a few minutes. Needle stays threaded longer when glued.
2. Lace. A right-handed person generally works from left to right. Always work from what is determined to be the right side of the project. Lacing on right side is more attractive. Straighten lace before pulling tight to avoid twists in the lace. Lace can be run out between fingers before putting in hole, to ensure straight lace. Length of lace should not be longer than an arm's length.
3. End lace. On coming to lace end bring lace to underneath side, cut to ½-inch length, and glue to leather. To end project, finish lace so ending cannot be seen, bring ends to underside of leather, and glue. To lace a corner, lace in the same way but go in one or more holes twice to cover corner.

Popular lacing methods

1. Loop stitch. Loop lace in hole and over edge, repeat.
2. Single buttonhole stitch. Put needle in hole, take needle under one lace at leather edge, enter next hole in leather, and so forth.
3. Double buttonhole stitch. Put needle in hole, take needle under two laces at leather edge, repeat, put needle in next hole.

Skills

1. Manual dexterity for detail work and holding needle.
2. Mental capacity to remember and repeat steps.
3. Fairly good eyesight, although touch can be used often.
Thus, the activity provides arm and finger exercise, promotes eye-hand coordination, and stimulates the mind in the step-by-step process.

Adaptations

For one-handed person, clamp work in a vise.

Choose lacing method person is capable of:
    simple (loop) to more complex (buttonhole).

For a longer, more complete leather project, leather can be purchased and resident can cut leather for billfold, for example, punch holes, and assemble. Leather tooling can also be done. These adaptations require other tools and skills than those listed.

figure 52
checklist for
making recipe or
card holders

CHECKLIST FOR MAKING RECIPE OR CARD HOLDERS

Materials

Pine pieces: several ¼-inch pieces, one 3-inch by 2-inch piece, one 1½-inch by 3½-inch piece angled to a 2-inch side
One clip-type wooden clothespin
Two small brads
Glue

Steps

1. Sand all surfaces.

2. Attach angled piece to center of long piece with two small brads in upright position.

3. Glue clothespin along angle with clip ½ inch beyond back edge of angled piece.

4. Spray or brush paint with enamel in any color.

5. Decorate side of upright with any small flowers, pictures, drawings, and so forth desired.

6. Add a typed card to clip as follows:
   This is quite a gadget,
       as you can plainly see.
   You can leave a note on it,
       or read a recipe.
   It's a great reminder,
       keeps you on the ball.
   As far as handy gadgets go,
       this is the handiest of all.

**figure 53
checklist for
making greeting cards**

CHECKLIST FOR MAKING GREETING CARDS

Materials

Tissues (white or colored)
Waxed paper
Pressed flowers or leaves
Cutouts from cards (holiday or other special occasion)
Glitter, sequins, or other decorations.
Glue
Plain paper (white or colored) for insert page
Newspaper
Thumbtacks
Cork board
Small paint brush
Scissors or pinking shears
Ruler
Pencil
Iron

Steps

1. Place waxed paper, cut to approximate size of card desired, on newspaper. Attach to table surface with tacks. (A piece of paper cut to exact size may be used under waxed paper as a guide.)

2. Arrange a design of pressed flowers or leaves for each side of the card.

3. Place one layer of tissue on top of the design and replace tacks to hold tissue.

4. Apply diluted glue (one part glue, one part water) to entire tissue surface with brush. Use a dabbing technique to avoid tearing tissue.

5. Sprinkle glitter or other decorations on top of glue.

6. Set card, still on newspaper, out to dry.

7. When it is dry, press card with warm iron. (Paper can be placed over and under the card to act as an absorbent and to protect iron.)

8. Measure card and cut to exact size with scissors or pinking shears.

9. Cut plain paper to size to make insert page for written greeting.

10. Match to envelope.

figure 54
checklist for
making wastebaskets

CHECKLIST FOR MAKING WASTEBASKETS

Materials

Large boxes, five-gallon ice cream containers, throwaway paint buckets,
    old wastebaskets
Wallpaper paste
Old sheets, terry cloth, or any textured cloth
Poster paint or enamel

Steps

1. Tear material into strips of usable size.
2. Dip strips in wallpaper paste mixed with water to the consistency of
    heavy cream.
3. Do not allow strips to be more than just saturated, as drying time is
    dependent on number of layers and thickness of material.
4. Line inside of container and entire outside if desired.
5. Paste strips to containers, forming ribbons, loops, bows, flowers, or
    whatever desired.
6. Set aside to dry thoroughly.
7. Use spray paint or poster paint to color desired areas. Be careful if using
    poster paint not to get material wet enough to sag from original design.
8. If poster paint is used, cover completely with a sealing spray of clear
    shellac or plastic.

figure 55
checklist for
making cannisters

CHECKLIST FOR MAKING CANNISTERS

Materials

Coffee can or shortening can of any size with plastic lid
Burlap, rickrack, ribbon, trim for lid
Glue
Spray paint

Steps

1. Spray-paint outside of can in color to cover printing.
2. Measure circumference and height of can, cut burlap to fit with ½-inch
    overlap on ends, glue to can, coming just to the rim at top and bottom.
3. Add desired trim to outside, making sure it will not bind under the
    plastic lid. (Put the lid on to measure the top edge of trim.)
4. Cut burlap to fit inside circle of lid. Glue on.
5. Choose and glue on coordinating trim, ribbons, bows, bells, fruit, flowers,
    or Christmas ornaments.
6. Punch holes in lid. Sew or wire through while holding down trim. Wires or
    stitches can be hidden by gluing another circle of burlap on the underside.
7. For kitchen cannisters, it is desirable to put a second plastic lid on the
    bottom to prevent rusting and scratching of surfaces. Be sure lower edge of
    trim is above rim of lid used on bottom.

**figure 56
checklist for making
pinecone flowers**

CHECKLIST FOR MAKING PINECONE FLOWERS

Materials

Pinecones
Poster paint
Florist wire
Florist tape
Florist picks

Steps

1. Slice pinecones through, making flower forms.
2. Wire "flowers" to picks; wrap wire with tape.
3. Paint in vivid colors.
4. Spray a sealer on flowers to preserve.
5. To give contrasting texture, some flowers can be shattered so the edges are fuzzy by crushing the petals carefully with pliers.
6. Arrange picks in a vase or bowl; attractively fill in with artificial pine.

**figure 57
checklist for making
flower plaques**

CHECKLIST FOR MAKING FLOWER PLAQUES

Materials

Pine boards, 3½ inches by 2½ inches (wood from orange crates is very good)
Straw flowers or dried grasses
Clear spray shellac, plastic, or varnish
Glue
Burlap or felt ribbon
Hangers

Steps

1. Sand all surfaces, rounding edges.
2. Glue on freeform design with grasses and flowers. Many design materials can be used, such as felt flowers, pinecones, papier-mâché forms, beads, and buttons.
3. Spray on several coats of shellac to bring out grain of wood and brighten colors.
4. Attach hangers.
5. Thumb tack to ribbon in series of three, if desired.
6. Use a rod sewn into the top hem or fasten to ring for hanging.
7. Fringe bottom edge of burlap, if used.

**figure 58
example of bylaws of
the residents' council**

BYLAWS OF THE RESIDENTS' COUNCIL

Article I: Name

The name of the organization shall be the Residents' Council.

Article II: Objective

The objective of the Residents' Council shall be to act as a self-governing body formulated to present questions and suggestions of the residents to the administration and staff and to promote the active involvement of the residents in every phase of life in the nursing home and in the community.

Article III: Officers

Section 1:   Officers
             The officers of the council shall be president, vice-president, and secretary.

Section 2:   Election
             Officers of the council shall be elected by individual vote of the council membership by secret ballot. All officers shall hold office for a period of one year beginning July 1 of each year. All officers may hold the same office for consecutive years provided they have been reelected.

Section 3:   Eligibility and qualifications
             Any member of the council in good standing is eligible.

Section 4:   Duties of officers
             A. President
                1. The president shall guide and conduct the activities of the council.
                2. The president shall preside at all meetings of the council.
                3. The president shall have the power to call special meetings of the members if there is a need, or of any committee of the council.
                4. The president shall appoint the chairman of any special committee.
             B. Vice-president
                1. The vice-president shall assume the duties of the president when the president is unable to act.
                2. The vice-president shall assume any duties assigned by the president.
             C. Secretary
                1. The secretary shall see that members are notified of the time and place of all meetings.
                2. The secretary shall take the minutes at all meetings.

Article IV: Committees

Section 1:   Committee chairmen shall appoint as many members as are necessary to carry on the work of the committee. Each committee chairman shall submit a report of the activities of the committee at the monthly meeting.

figure 58 (cont.)

Section 2: The building and grounds committee shall make a tour of regular inspection and report its findings. This report should include information relating to the general appearance, cleanliness and sanitation, and safety of the nursing home.

Section 3: The education committee shall suggest topics for classes, lectures, demonstrations, workshops, exhibits, films and slides, discussion groups, and other such activities.

Section 4: The history committee shall gather and disseminate historical information of interest to residents.

Section 5: The food committee shall obtain the general reaction of other residents to the food and service, investigate complaints, and discuss problems with the dietitian.

Section 6: The recreation committee shall work with the activity director in formulating, carrying out, and evaluating the monthly program.

Section 7: The religion committee shall assist in determining and carrying out the formalized chaplaincy program of the nursing home.

Section 8: The welcoming committee shall call on new residents in order to welcome them. The committee shall, in addition, sponsor a tea for new residents to be held every other month.

Article V: Meetings

Section 1: Monthly meetings
There shall be a meeting of the council on the first Tuesday of each month unless otherwise announced.

Section 2: Special meetings
Special meetings of the council may be called at any time by the president.

Section 3: Notice
Notice of meetings shall be published in the calendar of events. All members shall be reminded of the time, date, and place over the public address system on the date of meeting.

Article VI: Nominations and Elections

Section 1: Nominations
All council members will have the right to nominate candidates at a council meeting one month prior to election of officers.

Section 2: Elections
A. Elections will take place at the regularly scheduled monthly meeting following the nomination of candidates for office.
B. Election of officers will take place by secret ballot.
C. The newly elected officers will assume their duties at this meeting.

Article VII: Amendments

These bylaws may be amended by a two-thirds vote of the voting members present at any regular or special meeting, provided all members have been notified of the proposed amendments one week in advance.

**figure 58
(cont.)**

Article VIII: Agenda

The following agenda shall be used for regular meetings of the council:

I. Minutes
   A. Discussion
   B. Approval
II. Old or unfinished business
III. Committee reports
   A. Building and grounds
   B. Education
   C. History
   D. Food
   E. Recreation
   F. Religion
   G. Welcoming
IV. New business
V. Adjournment

**figure 59
example of
class outline**

OUTLINE FOR MUSIC CLASS

First Class: Music Trends: 16th through 20th Centuries

I. Introduction
   A. Introduction of instructor
   B. Explanation of plans for this class and following classes
II. Brief explanation of what a music trend is and how to recognize one
   A. Renaissance period
      1. Explain characteristics of this period.
      2. Play an example: *Sonata Piano Forte,* by Giovanni Gabrieli.
      3. Discuss the piece and give opinions.
   B. Baroque period
      1. Explain why this period evolved and its characteristics.
      2. Play an example: Cantata No. 63, *Christen, atzet diesen Tag,* by Johann Sebastian Bach.
      3. Briefly discuss Bach and his works.
   C. Classical period
      1. Explain what *classical* really means and why this period was labeled as such.
      2. Play an example: *Concerto for Piano and Orchestra in D Minor,* by Wolfgang Amadeus Mozart.
      3. Discuss what a concerto is and some things about Mozart's life.
   D. Romantic period
      1. Explain why this period was influenced by other fields of learning.
      2. Play an example: *Symphony No. 1 in C Minor,* opus 68, by Johannes Brahms.
      3. Discuss why Brahms was so characteristic of this period.

This outline was excerpted from an outline for a music appreciation course developed and conducted at Swope Ridge Health Care Center through a cooperative arrangement with the University of Missouri at Kansas City, School of Education.

**figure 59
(cont.)**

    E. 20th-century music
1. Explain why this century's music sounds so different.
2. Play an example: *The Rites of Spring,* by Igor Stravinsky.
3. Discuss what lies ahead for music.

III. Conclusion
Open discussion: Listeners are urged to ask questions about what they've heard or about other aspects of music.

Second Class: A History of the Folk Song

I. Introduction
    A. Definition of the folk song
    B. Explanation of why it is so important

II. Various stages in the development of the folk song
    A. People coming to the new world, circa 1600
    B. Early American songs
        1. Political
        2. Example: "Liberty Song"
    C. First American songs
        1. Songs of morality
        2. Henry Russell, composer
    D. Working Americans
        1. Move to the West
        2. Examples: "Skip to My Lou," "A Shantyman's Life," "Oh, Susanna"
    E. Influence of Civil War
        1. William Steffe, composer
        2. Example: "Battle Hymn of the Republic"
    F. Opening of the West
        1. Railroad workers' songs
        2. Cowboys' tunes
    G. Plantation workers' style
    H. Sentimental era, circa 1890
        1. Mother theme
        2. Sentimentality
        3. Example: "Daisy Bell"
    I. Popular songs of the 1900s
        1. Tin Pan Alley
        2. Song pluggers
        3. Ragtime: Irving Berlin
        4. Blues: Thomas C. Handy
        5. Modern jazz: Paul Whiteman, Ferde Grofé, George Gershwin
        6. Swing: Duke Ellington
    J. Instruments applicable to folk song

Third Class: The Heritage of the Hymn

I. Introduction
    A. The first hymn (from the eighth and ninth centuries)
    B. Setting the Psalms to music

**figure 59
(cont.)**

C. Important composers of early hymns
   1. Thomas Sternhold
   2. Isaac Watts
   3. James Montgomery

II. Contents of a hymnal
   A. Subject-matter organization versus seasonal organization
   B. Tune names
   C. Meter and pulse

III. Examples of hymns and their derivations
   A. "A Mighty Fortress Is Our God" (early 1500s)
   B. "All People That on Earth Do Dwell" (16th century)
   C. "Fairest Lord Jesus" (1850)
   D. "For All the Saints" (19th century)
   E. "All Hail the Power of Jesus' Name" (18th century)
   F. "O God, Our Help in Ages Past" (17th century)

The fourth, fifth, sixth, and seventh classes cover, respectively, the music of Kern and Gershwin, the waltz, the carol, and musical instruments and their uses.

**figure 60
checklist for
conducting the
'tonight' show**

CHECKLIST FOR CONDUCTING THE 'TONIGHT' SHOW

Preparation

1. Invite local celebrities, or celebrities on road shows, and individuals or groups with interesting backgrounds to be guests on the "Tonight" show. At least three different guests are desirable to offer variety. Guests might include a performer, zoo director, sports personality, writer, and so forth.

2. Arrange a small band or at least a pianist to provide music during the program and to participate in the "Stump the Band" activity.

3. Prepare a set similar to that of the "Tonight" show, with a desk for the person who is playing the role of Johnny, chair and couch, microphone, colorful background, and possibly a large plant.

4. The person who will be Johnny should watch the "Tonight" show several times to get a good understanding of his role. Purchase one of Johnny Carson's books, such as *Happiness Is a Dry Martini,* or design a cape and hat such as Johnny wears when he portrays "Karnac," and make up answers and questions.

5. Arrange for a staff member or volunteer to be the announcer, to play the role of Ed McMahon.

6. Have a few prizes available for audience contestants who participate in "Stump the Band."

7. Plan an area for guests to wait comfortably prior to being introduced. Have a volunteer host or hostess available.

8. Prepare some questions and topics for the interview period with the guests.

Activity

1. Announcer introduces "Johnny."

2. Band or pianist begins playing something peppy; audience applauds.

3. Johnny enters, gives the signal to stop the music, and either is prepared with a brief monolog or just welcomes the audience to the "Tonight" show. Johnny announces guests for the evening.

4. Johnny sits down, chats briefly with the announcer, and then either reads from the book or does the "Karnac" routine.

5. Johnny introduces the first guest. If he or she is an entertainer, the guest should perform.

6. Johnny talks with the first guest for 5 to 10 minutes and then introduces the next guest. They talk for 5 to 10 minutes.

7. Guests who have been interviewed are welcome to stay and take part in the conversations with other guests, or they may leave.

8. A humorous commercial should be given some time during the program.

9. Johnny goes into the audience to play "Stump the Band." Only three or four participants should be used.

10. Johnny returns to the stage and introduces the last guest. They talk for 5 to 10 minutes.

11. Johnny thanks all of the guests, thanks the audience, and says goodnight.

12. The band ends with a number.

13. A few days later thank you letters should be sent to all guests.

**figure 61
checklist for
group exercise
program**

CHECKLIST FOR GROUP EXERCISE PROGRAM

1. Sit straight. Put arms in front (shoulder level), arms straight out to the sides, arms over the head, arms down to the sides. After the demonstration, count as the group does the exercises: 1 - 2 - 3 - 4. Do this exercise about seven times.

2. Breathe deeply, sit tall, inhale slowly through the nose, hold a second or two, exhale *slowly* through the mouth with lips pursed—like blowing out a candle. Blow out as much air as possible. Hold a second or two. Inhale as before. (It is important that the person exhales as much as *possible*.)

3. Start with arms straight out, fingers extended, palms down. Bend elbows on the count of one, and, as elbows are bent, flex the fingers to make a fist, turning forearms so that the closed fists are toward the face. Extend elbows on two, opening and turning hands to palms facing the floor again. Repeat several times: 1 - 2, 1 - 2, and so on.

4. Breathe deeply two times.

5. Make a fist, straighten the fingers. Start with palms down, as the fist is made; turn hands to palms up. Repeat 8 to 10 times: 1 - 2, 1 - 2, and so on. Exercises 3 and 5 are similar.

6. Breathe deeply two times.

7. Put both legs out straight, lower them to the floor: 1 - 2, 1 - 2. Repeat.

8. Breathe deeply two times.

9. Spread fingers wide apart, pull them back together keeping fingers extended: 1 - 2, 1 - 2. Repeat 10 times.

10. Breathe deeply two times.

11. Touch thumbs to little fingers, then to each other finger. Open thumb wide each time before going to the next finger: 1 - 2 - 3 - 4. Repeat 10 times.

12. Breathe deeply two times.

13. Sit tall, look down at lap, look over right shoulder at floor behind, look down at lap, look over left shoulder at floor behind. Do this three or four times each side.

14. Look down at right hip, look over left shoulder at the ceiling. Repeat four times.

15. Open mouth wide and hold it—about seven seconds. Do only once.

16. Tighten all the muscles in the front of the neck by lowering chin slightly and tensing the muscles. Hold for about 10 seconds. Do only once.

17. Relieve the tension. Wrinkle up the nose and hold it for six to seven seconds. Do only once.

18. Make big eyes, don't blink, look from side to side, up and down and around. Blink.

Exercises developed by Emma Stephens, R.N., RPT, Swope Ridge.

**figure 62
checklist for
organizing a
bunco game**

CHECKLIST FOR ORGANIZING A BUNCO GAME

Materials
Three dice for each table
Scorecards
Pencils

Steps

1. Residents are divided into groups. Each group sits at a table and receives three dice.
2. One person in each group rolls one die to determine the trump point.
3. A player then throws all three dice in an attempt to make points. One point is scored every time a trump is thrown, 5 points for 3 of any kind but trump, and 32 points (Bunco) for 3 trump.

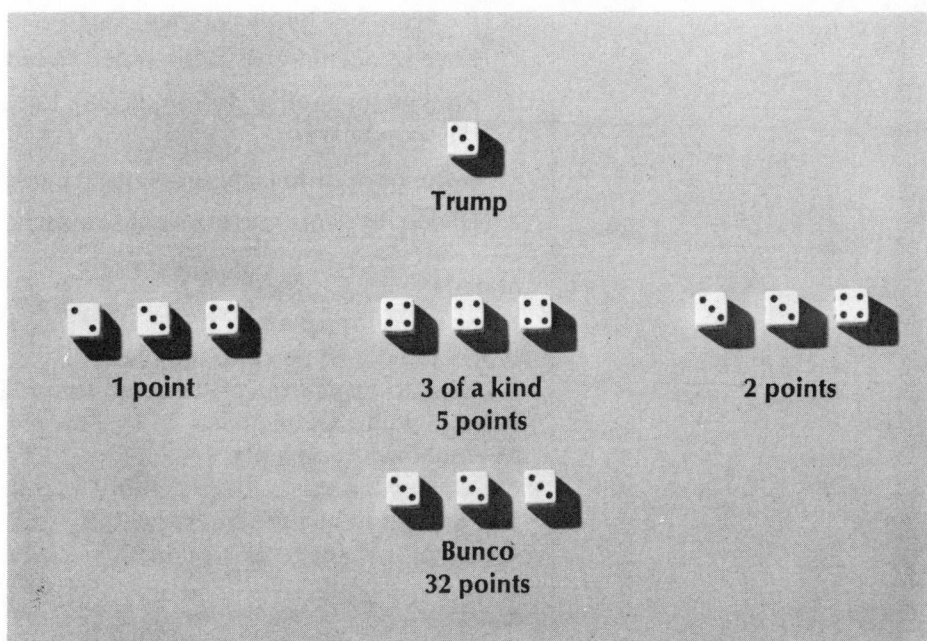

4. The player continues to throw the dice as long as points are scored. If not, the dice are passed to the player to the left.
5. The game continues until a player gets a Bunco. At this time one die is thrown to determine another trump and the game begins again.
6. A prize is awarded at the end of the game for the person scoring the most points.

**figure 63
checklist for playing
'two for the money'**

CHECKLIST FOR PLAYING 'TWO FOR THE MONEY'

Preparation

1. Make up categories and select examples, such as:
    Magazines *(Time)*
    Flowers (rose)
    Transportation (automobile)
    Sports (baseball)
    Fish (trout)
    Languages (English)
    Birds (robin)
    Capitals (Washington, DC)
    State capitals (Jefferson City, MO)
    Planets (Earth)
    Birthstones (ruby)
    Broadway musicals *(Oklahoma)*

2. Have someone serve as the expert to judge incorrect answers or repeats.

3. Arrange for another person to keep track of the score and to record on the scoreboard.

4. Invite from six to eight residents to participate.

5. Divide residents into teams of two each.

Materials

Name cards for panelists
Braces to hold name cards upright
Scoreboard made from posterboard (or use blackboard)
A watch with a second hand
Microphones, if possible
One long table
Bell or horn to be used by expert
Prizes for winning team (optional)

Rules

1. Each team has 30 seconds to identify as many examples as possible in each category.

2. Panelists must answer alternately.

3. If an incorrect answer is given, the team has no more time for that category.

4. If a repeat answer is given, the team has no more time for that category.

5. The score is determined by the number of correct answers times the number of correct answers in the preceding round. For example, in the first round, 9 points are scored. In the second round, if 8 points are scored, the number of points would be 8 times 9, or 72 points. In the third round, the number of correct answers would be multiplied by 8.

**figure 63
(cont.)**

Steps

1. Introduce the scorekeeper and the expert.

2. Provide general information and explain the rules.
    Ask the audience not to call out answers.

3. Introduce the first team.

4. Hold a brief interview with each team member.

5. Give the first example. When the team begins, start the 30-second time
    period.

6. Go through four categories with the team.

7. Follow the same procedure with each team.

8. Present prizes, if desired and feasible.

**figure 64
checklist for playing
'what's my line?'**

CHECKLIST FOR PLAYING 'WHAT'S MY LINE?'

Preparation

1. Invite five guests from the community to appear before a panel of
    residents.

2. Ask the guests not to wear clothing that would identify their occupations.

3. One of the five invited guests should be known to all the panelists by
    name, face, or reputation; a celebrated personality of stage, screen, radio,
    television, or sports would fit this part. This person is designated as the
    "Mystery Guest," and he must not let any of the panelists know of his
    presence. When he appears before the panel, he will disguise his voice
    and panelists will be blindfolded.

4. Meet with the guests for 15 minutes before the program to discuss
    the rules, explain the scoring system, and answer any questions.

5. The day before the program, select four residents to be panelists.
    Maintain at least two permanent panelists; the other two may alternate
    with substitutes.

6. Meet with the panelists sometime before the program.
    a. Distribute a list of suggested questions.
    b. Develop an understanding of the general aspects of questioning.
    c. Explain that questions must be phrased so that they can be answered
        yes or *no*.
    d. Have a practice session using occupations that will not be represented.

Materials

Name cards for panelists and moderator
Braces to hold name cards upright
Corsages and boutonnieres for guests (optional)
Four eye masks for panelists to wear during appearance of mystery guest
Flip cards numbered 1 through 10 to indicate the number of *no* answers
    received by the panel
Two blackboards and two pieces of chalk, one to use for guests to sign in
    and one to show audience the guest's occupation

**figure 64
(cont.)**

One long table for panelists
One small table or desk for moderator and guest
Clock or watch with a second hand
Microphones if possible
Sample question sheets for panel members

Rules

1. Panelists are told whether guest is salaried or self-employed and whether his occupation involves a service or a product.

2. Questions must be phrased so that they can be answered *yes* or *no*.

3. A panelist may continue to ask questions until he receives a *no* answer or until he runs out of questions.

4. Each *no* answer counts 1 point against the panel. If the panel receives 10 points before it guesses the occupation, the panel loses the game.

5. Panelists may request a consultation period of 30 seconds, which is granted at the discretion of the moderator. Otherwise, the panelists work individually.

Steps

1. Give a brief description of the game. Introduce the panelists. Ask the audience not to give away the guest's occupation.

2. Ask the first guest to enter, sign in, and sit down.

3. Have a staff member or volunteer write the guest's "line" on a blackboard visible only to the audience.

4. Introduce the guest to the panel. Ask the first panelist to begin the questioning.

5. Follow the rules of the game.

6. Flip over a card for every question receiving a *no* answer.

7. Following the identification of the guest's occupation (either guessed by the panel or told by the guest if the panel is stumped), ask the guest to give a brief description of his work.

8. If the guest brought along friends or relatives who are seated in the audience, introduce them to the residents.

9. Thank the guest for participating and encourage applause when he leaves.

10. Follow the same procedure for each guest except the mystery guest. Prior to his entrance, panelists should be blindfolded. The scoring procedure can be changed for the mystery guest, having each panelist in turn ask only one question at a time until the guest is identified or until 10 questions have received a *no* answer.

**figure 65
example of
list of
ideas for a
lecture series**

IDEAS FOR A LECTURE SERIES

Germany: Its Land and People
  Deputy Consul of Germany

Our Churches: Where Are They Going?
  Chaplain, United Council of Churches

The Family of Yesterday and Tomorrow
  Director of Family Studies Center, University

The Mormon Church
  Church Member

The People of Africa
  Peace Corps Volunteer

What's New in Medicine?
  Assistant Director of Artificial Kidney Project, Hospital

The Montessori Teaching Method
  Teacher, "Little Red School House" Montessori School

What's New in Education?
  Assistant Professor, University

Cast Your Ballot
  President, League of Women Voters

A Look at New Books
  Catalog Information Department, Public Library

What's Cooking?
  Home Economist, University Extension Center

Spanish Influence in Our City
  Honorary Vice-Consul of Spain

What's New in Dentistry?
  Chairman, Department of Preventive Dentistry, University

Tornadoes
  Meteorologist, U.S. Air Force

Drug Abuse Control
  Case Officer, U.S. Bureau of Narcotics and Dangerous Drugs

The Changing Central City
  Community Developer, City Hall

How Good Is Your Reading?
  Director, Reading Center, University

The Catholic Church in Renewal
  Priest

What's New in Sports?
  Professional Football Player and Television Sports Director

**figure 65
(cont.)**

Art Forms as Aid to Worship
  Vicar, Church

History of Life on Earth
  Member, Earth Science Club

Frauds and Swindles
  Staff Member, Better Business Bureau

Dolls from around the world
  Resident, Nursing Home

This is God's World
  Member, Audubon Nature Club

The World Population Dilemma
  Representative, Planned Parenthood Association

Early Days in Our City
  City Archivist and Historian

The Incredible Machine: Telephone of the Future
  Speakers' Bureau, Telephone Company

Law Enforcement in Your Area
  Lieutenant, City Police Department

The Jewish Religion
  Rabbi

New Frontiers in Education
  President, Junior College

Your Medicare
  Representative, Social Security Administration

The History and Mystery of Your Name (Genealogy)
  Hobbyist

Indians of North America and Their Artifacts
  Member, Archaeological Society

United Fund
  Speakers' Bureau, United Fund

Unity among Christians
  Past National President, United Church Women

The Changing Face of Our City
  Author and Lecturer

Famous Families of Our City
  Librarian or Archivist

Rehabilitation in Federal Penitentiaries
  Criminologist

**figure 65
(cont.)**

John Neihardt and His Lyric Poetry
　　Associate Feature Editor, City Newspaper

The Beauty of Stamps
　　Regional Director, American Association of Retired People

Fencing
　　Member, Amateur Fencers League of America

Great Books
　　Discussion Club Leader

Victorian Costumes
　　Costume Curator, City Museum

Growing African Violets
　　Hobbyist

Canine Obedience Demonstration
　　Member, Obedience School

The Model Cities Program
　　Specialist, Institute for Community Studies

Forty Years Ago
　　Librarian, City Newspaper

What's New in Physics?
　　Physicist

Indian Culture
　　Historian

Wood Carving
　　Hobbyist

General Police Training
　　Police Officer

Unity Principles
　　Minister

Jewish Holy Days
　　Rabbi

The Philippines and Their Customs
　　Traveler

Veterans Day
　　Official of the Veterans of Foreign Wars

Leather Work
　　Representative of Leather Company

**figure 65
(cont.)**

The Development of the Civic Center
    Public Relations Staff Member of Local Firm

City History of Crime and Politics
    Police Officer

The Anatomy of Loneliness
    Psychologist, Hospital

Photography as a Hobby
    Advertising Specialist

Public Relations in Politics
    Judge

**figure 66
checklist for
organizing an indoor
gardening project**

CHECKLIST FOR ORGANIZING AN INDOOR GARDENING PROJECT

Materials

Containers with lids
Charcoal or pebbles
Soil mixture
Small plants
Empty spray bottle

Steps

1. Select containers (one for each participating resident) that will be used to house the minigardens. Good containers include glass casserole dishes, brandy snifters, clear plastic bread or cake holders, or aquariums. Each container must have a clear lid.
2. Purchase or gather enough charcoal or pebbles to cover the bottom of each container.
3. Purchase enough soil mixture and vermiculite or screened sphagnum moss to cover the base, approximately ½ inch of each for every container.
4. Have each resident place a layer of charcoal or pebbles in the bottom of his container for drainage.
5. Have each resident cover this layer with the soil mixture.
6. Have each resident add ½ inch of vermiculite or screened sphagnum moss, making sure there is room left for the plants to grow.
7. Have each resident plant some suitable plants.
8. Have each resident water his terrarium with a spray bottle.

**figure 67
checklist for
organizing an outdoor
gardening project**

CHECKLIST FOR ORGANIZING AN OUTDOOR GARDENING PROJECT

Materials

Hand diggers, spades, tablespoons
Sprinkling can
Plastic gloves
Aprons
Plants
Plant food
Soil mixture (one gallon per empty half barrel)
Miscellaneous small rocks
Half barrels or other containers for soil

Steps

1. Assess the need for plants.

2. Obtain plants from nurseries or garden clubs. Suitable flowers include petunias, pansies, geraniums, and marigolds; suitable foliage includes coleus, Joseph's coat, and ferns.

3. Give each resident a half barrel in which the flowers will be planted.

4. Have residents prepare soil the day before planting. The soil should be loosened all the way down to the barrel bottom. The drainage hole should be open. Stones can be added to bottom for better drainage. For best results soil should be removed from barrels, a layer of small rocks should be placed on bottom, and the soil should be placed on top of rocks.

5. Have residents add dry plant food mixture to the soil.

6. Have residents plant the flowers or foliage that has been designated for them.

7. Barrels should be spaced so that there is enough room around each for wheelchairs. Weather permitting, residents can work on patios; in bad weather, they can work in halls or hobby areas.

8. Residents capable of watering and tending to barrels should have assignments for summer months. Volunteers need to be assigned to follow up, assist residents, and determine any later needs for this project.

Note: For planting in barrels and miscellaneous other planting, a staff member plus several volunteers are required to assist and direct residents. Have several residents to help at each barrel.

figure 68
checklist for
organizing a
birthday party

CHECKLIST FOR ORGANIZING A BIRTHDAY PARTY

Preparation

1. Set a date and time for the party.
2. Determine the theme of the party.
3. Schedule entertainment. Try to arrange it to coincide with the theme.
4. Get a list of residents who will have birthdays during the month.
5. Send out invitations to close relatives of, or the party responsible for, each birthday person.
6. Select and order refreshments, including a cake, from the kitchen.
7. Schedule the staff members or volunteers who will be required to help during the party.
8. Make birthday cards, with the help of residents.
9. Write personalized verses for the inside of each card for each birthday person, with the help of residents.
10. Make artificial corsages and boutonnieres for the birthday persons.
11. Decide if the party will include games, music, readings, and so forth, and make necessary preparations.
12. Prepare decorations, with the help of residents, in line with the party theme.
13. Consider a special announcement for the party.
14. Determine the room arrangement.
15. Immediately before the party, pick up refreshments, arrange and hang decorations, and arrange the area. Place materials and props needed for games and the cards and artificial flowers near the announcer.

Steps

1. Seat the birthday persons near the front of the room.
2. Welcome those who have come to the party.
3. Introduce the first birthday person and assist him to the front. Read aloud the verse that has been prepared for that person. Ask the person to face the audience, and give him the card and corsage or boutonniere. Have the pianist play "Happy Birthday" and the audience sing. Have the person return to his seat. Repeat this step with each person being honored.
4. If planned, introduce the resident who will read the horoscope for the month.
5. Conduct any games or activities that have been planned.
6. Introduce any entertainment scheduled for the party.
7. Cut the cake and serve refreshments. Allow other residents to help, if possible.
8. End the party.

**figure 69
checklist for
organizing a
fashion show**

CHECKLIST FOR ORGANIZING A FASHION SHOW

Preparation

1. Contact residents who can participate and invite them to be in the fashion show. Ask them what they might wear.

2. Contact the family or friends of participating residents and invite them to participate or attend.

3. Set a deadline for fashion show participants to announce what they have decided to wear. Probably 15 to 25 entries would be adequate.

4. Write a brief description of each fashion entry and type or write these descriptions in the order in which they will be announced.

5. Order refreshments for after the show; arrange for residents to serve.

6. Decorate the area where the show will be presented.

7. Inform the "models" of the plan and tell them whom they will follow. Have someone work with this group in order to have the next person ready.

Steps

1. Welcome the audience and present some generalizations about the fashions to be modeled.

2. Introduce the first model and describe what he or she is wearing.

3. Continue to introduce the models in the order planned.

4. When the show is over, thank the models and serve the refreshments.

**figure 70
checklist for
organizing a
watermelon feast**

CHECKLIST FOR ORGANIZING A WATERMELON FEAST

1. Order enough watermelons and cantaloupes to serve at least two pieces to each resident.

2. Plan a demonstration of some type (perhaps a canine obedience demonstration) to be presented prior to serving the melon.

3. After the demonstration or other activity, cut and serve the melon. Seat residents in a way that encourages them to visit informally with one another while eating.

4. If desired, have a watermelon eating contest with ¼ of a slice for each participant. Present a homemade badge ("Watermelon Eating Champion") to the winner.

figure 71
checklist for
organizing a picnic

CHECKLIST FOR ORGANIZING A PICNIC

Preparation

1. Set date and time.
2. Invite residents.
3. Determine the number attending.
4. Select the appropriate area.
5. Select the menu and requisition food, supplies, and equipment needed.
6. Plan activities, considering residents' limitations.
7. Prepare decorations.
8. Arrange for staff members or volunteers to assist.

Materials

Serving table
Tables and chairs for residents
Napkins, bibs or aprons
Plates, cups, eating utensils
Serving utensils
Paper towels
Matches
Aluminum foil
Table cover
Grill or grills
Charcoal
Charcoal lighter
Water container (for the fire)
Waste containers
Food:
    Hamburgers or hot dogs
    Buns
    Catsup, mustard, relish, onions, pickles
    Salad, tomatoes
    Baked beans
    Potato chips, pretzels
    Punch, tea, coffee
    Sugar, cream
    Salt, pepper
    Dessert (ice cream, cookies, watermelon)

Steps

1. Organize equipment several hours ahead of time. Move it outside and set up the area.
2. Start the fire.
3. Bring out the food.
4. Set up the serving table in an organized way so that a person can start at one end and have everything on his plate when he gets to the other end.

**figure 71
(cont.)**

5. Escort residents to the picnic area and seat them.

6. Prepare the plates and serve them. Have a resident pour drinks while others serve.

7. After everyone has eaten, begin cleaning up.

8. Begin activity if planned. Appropriate activities include skits with residents participating, group singing, and games such as croquet.

9. After the activity, escort residents back into building.

10. Finish cleaning up.

**figure 72
checklist for
organizing a
shuffleboard game**

CHECKLIST FOR ORGANIZING A SHUFFLEBOARD GAME

Preparation

1. Select a tile floor area on which masking tape can be placed.

2. Tape two triangles on the floor, with the tips pointing away from the participants. The two triangles should be approximately six feet apart to allow for movement of wheelchairs.

3. Mark numbers in spaces within the triangles, as shown:

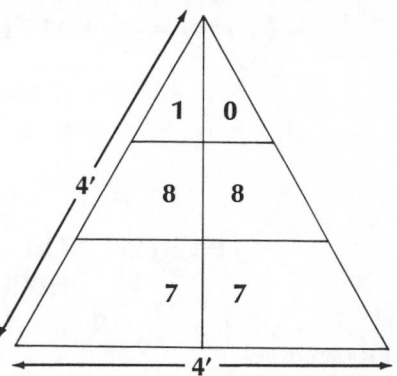

4. Set out equipment (cues and discs).

Steps

1. Arrange players so that all can see the triangle.

2. Present a brief explanation of the rules:
   a. A disc on the line doesn't count.
   b. A player may knock off an opponent's disc to his own advantage.
   c. Scoring: Points are given as marked in triangle. Points are totaled for each team. The winner is the first player to score 21 points or whatever total has been designated.

3. Let each player practice with the cue and disc. Because residents have a limited power and energy output, they should not stand too many feet away from the scoring area.

4. Divide the residents into two teams. Play a game.

5. Play for either an established length of time or a certain score.

CHECKLIST FOR ORGANIZING A CASTING AND FISHING ACTIVITY

Preparation

1. Secure rods, reels, and taped hooks or weights. Bamboo poles can be used. Obtain minnows, worms, or other bait.

2. If fishing, allocate the fish in some manner. A nature center is an excellent source if its staff is notified at least one week ahead of time.

3. A pond, small swimming pool, or fountain arrangement is needed. Some form of antichlorine crystal should be added to the water before the fish are added.

4. Arrange for volunteers to assist.

Steps

1. Give instructions and stress safety.

2. Show the form in casting, wrist snap, and release.

3. Have participants practice casting. (When casting only, hooks should not be used.)

4. If fishing, direct residents to the location of the fish. If real fish are not available, use plastic magnetic fish and magnets tied to the lines.

CHECKLIST FOR ORGANIZING AN INDOOR HORSESHOE GAME

Preparation

1. Select a carpeted area for the game.

2. Obtain needed equipment: two stakes and four or more rubber horseshoes.

3. Secure the base of the stakes to the floor with heavy-duty tape to avoid tipping.

Steps

1. Have participants sit a reasonable distance from the stakes.

2. Explain the scoring procedure: a horseshoe landing within 6 inches of the stake counts 2 points, a horseshoe leaning on the stake counts 3 points, a ringer counts 5 points.

3. Have participants practice casting. (When casting only, hooks should not be used.)

4. Play several games and keep score. If desired, a tournament can be set up.

**figure 75
checklist for
organizing an indoor
bowling game**

CHECKLIST FOR ORGANIZING AN INDOOR BOWLING GAME

Preparation

1. Obtain needed equipment: a plastic bowling set and ball.

2. Arrange an alley about 10 feet long and 5 inches high with a backstop. A cardboard cutout can be constructed and taped to the floor.

3. Make scoring sheets and appoint someone to keep score.

4. Arrange for two other aides to spot pins and return the ball.

Steps

1. Arrange the residents so all can see the bowlers. Ask residents to volunteer to participate.

2. Explain that a rebounded ball does not count in knocking down the pins.

3. Have the participants practice.

4. Play a game of five lines and keep score. If desired, a tournament can be set up.

**figure 76
checklist for
organizing an indoor
golf game**

CHECKLIST FOR ORGANIZING AN INDOOR GOLF GAME

Preparation

1. Obtain golf clubs and balls. A public golf course is a good source.

2. Arrange some devices to shoot the balls into. These can be commercial or homemade.

3. Determine the area for the activity. A carpeted area is best.

4. Build some sort of backstop for the balls.

5. Construct various obstacle courses from boxes, cartons, bleach bottles, and wood. Four should be enough, depending on the space available.

Steps

1. Explain the game and stress safety.

2. Have the participants practice putting and swinging.

3. Have the participants go through the obstacle course with volunteers serving as caddies. They can also assist in scoring and pushing wheelchairs.

4. If necessary, a participant may move the ball slightly for a more advantageous position. A small move should be overlooked.

5. If the ball can overshoot the target, establish a boundary line rule. Possibly a penalty ball could be given or the player can start over on that hole.

6. If the activity seems popular, arrange for residents to go to a miniature golf course.

figure 77
example of
visitation card

Dear_____,
                    (Name of clergyman)

_____ was admitted to _____
        (Name of resident)   (Name of nursing home)

on _____. Your church has been designated as the spiritual
              (Date)

home of our new resident. We sincerely hope that you will call on your

parishioner at the first opportunity. Please call regularly at your convenience.

Sincerely,

_____
(Name of activity director or administrator)